THE TRANSFORMATION SERIES
Gay Hendricks, *General Editor*

Books in the Transformation Series explore the transitions
of human life and the possibilities for happier, more creative living
through the application of the psychology of adjustment

Books in the series:

gay hendricks

the centered teacher

awareness activities for teachers and their students

A SPECTRUM BOOK

PRENTICE-HALL, INC.
Englewood Cliffs, N.J. 07632

Library of Congress Cataloging in Publication Data

Hendricks, Gay
   The centered teacher.

   (The Transformation Series) (A Spectrum Book)
   Includes bibliographies.
   1.–Teaching. 2.–Self-perception in children.
I.–Title.
LB1025.2.H44   371.1′02   80-27817
ISBN 0-13-122234-1
ISBN 0-13-122226-0 (pbk.)

© 1981 by Prentice-Hall, Inc.
Englewood Cliffs, New Jersey 07632

A SPECTRUM BOOK

10 9 8 7 6 5 4 3 2 1

Printed in the United States of America

Editorial/production supervision and interior design by Cyndy Lyle

Manufacturing buyer: Cathie Lenard

Prentice-Hall International, Inc., *London*
Prentice-Hall of Australia Pty. Limited, *Sydney*
Prentice-Hall of Canada, Ltd., *Toronto*
Prentice-Hall of India Private Limited, *New Delhi*
Prentice-Hall of Japan, Inc., *Tokyo*
Prentice-Hall of Southeast Asia Pte. Ltd., *Singapore*
Whitehall Books Limited, *Wellington, New Zealand*

contents

centering and relaxation

centering in special education, reading, and administration

introduction

centering in special education

centering and reading

the centering principal

*This book is dedicated to Lynne Lumsden,
editor of gifted vision.*

Right education is to help you
find out for yourself what you really,
with all your heart, love to do.

J. Krishnamurti

preface

In the third grade we were told to stop using the pronoun *I* in our writing. My teachers meant well, I suppose; they were trying to encourage a more objective point-of-view. But now I regard the removal of my *I* as a symbol of much of what I found wanting in my education. *I* surgery takes the experiencer out of the picture, causing the validity of our personal experience to be denied. Perhaps our writing did become more objective, but it also lost much of its force, spark, and authenticity.

When I look back on my education, it is the personal touch, those moments in which I felt my sense of *I* enhanced, that stands out in my memory. For example, my second-grade teacher was cold and distant. I did the bare minimum work for her, and now cannot recall her name. My fourth-grade teacher, Miss Leonard, was warm and jolly, and put her hand on my shoulder when she passed by. I wrote essays for her, read a book a week, and even learned the rest of my multiplication tables. She touched me.

Sometimes a rare teacher can give us the gift of life itself. One of my professors in graduate school, Dwight Webb, mainly taught by sharing himself with his students. He talked easily about his feelings, thoughts, and the problems he encountered on his journey. Simply being around Dwight taught me that it was all right to be myself. Dwight encouraged me to open up to my feelings, to figure out what I wanted in life, to express my creativity, and to communicate in straightforward ways. By having the support in looking at the darker parts of myself, I came across light I had not seen before. At first the journey was hard; I had grown up in a world where big boys did not have feelings, much less show them. But Dwight inspired me. He was not afraid to cry or express joy around us, and he was more of a man than anyone I had ever met. It became impossible in his presence to hold on to the old wooden version of myself, so I let go and for the first time in my life felt fully alive. Joy entered my life, creativity began to flow, and though it took me years to clear up the painful details of my life, I can see that the moment of transformation took place when Dwight showed me that it was possible to be real.

Some years later I had a serendipitous merging of my own interests with what I perceived to be a need in education. I was in the habit of dropping by my daughter's first-grade classroom, where I took much delight in seeing twenty-five magnificent little people a-buzz with light, energy, and a touch of mischief. There I noticed a heavy emphasis on intellectual things, as opposed to kinesthetic, emotional, social, and artistic activities that would more clearly reflect the nature of six-year-olds. In other words, there was too much sitting and not enough dancing. About this same time I was beginning to feel the value of mind-body activities like meditation, relaxation training, creative movement, and guided fantasy. I was meditating regularly, and enjoying peace of mind instead of the rude, horn-honking traffic that had been in my consciousness before meditation. I began to wonder if we could create a place in education for a curriculum of activities that would serve the moving, feeling parts of us as well as the thinking.

Enter Jim Fadiman, who helped me take all these ferment-ing ideas and bottle the wine. Jim, whose genius is putting people in touch with their inner source of creativity, simply asked me what I most wanted to do. The moment he asked the question I knew what I wanted to do. I wanted to build a curriculum for the whole person. I also saw that in counseling and psychotherapy, my other area of interest, I wanted to discover the basic principles that generate transformation. With the help of colleagues like Tom Roberts, Russel Wills and Barry Weinhold, I set about the happy task of writing books such as the series of *Centering Books* and *Transpersonal Education*. The cycle that began with the question Jim asked now culminates with the present volume, the last book I anticipate writing in education. Now I plan to spend my research and writing time in psycho-therapy research, although I will continue to work with teachers at conferences and workshops.

At a lecture I estimated that it would take about twenty years for material such as that contained in the present book to become widely used in American education. At this the audience groaned. Why should it take so long to integrate innovations in the classroom, they asked. Personally I do not feel that twenty years is long. After all, material on communication skills like Tom Gordon's *Teacher Effectiveness Training* was known twenty-five years ago, but is only recently finding widespread use in education. Educational change is slow, perhaps for good reason. It takes a while to separate skills of enduring value from fads.

In the meantime we can take inspiration from knowing, now perhaps more than ever, that we work for the larger evolution of the planet. Twenty or two hundred years is an eyeblink in the larger view of things. It is quality and commit-ment, both timeless values, that determine the meaning of our gift to humanity and our children. If we know our hearts, and follow our paths with passion, then I believe we will only know good.

My best to you on that journey.

teaching
is centering

1

teaching and centering

A quiet, compassionate revolution is underway in education. It is a grassroots revolution led by teachers who have a deep commitment to their own evolution, and to the evolution of students and society. This movement views teaching as an opportunity for teachers to expand their consciousness while assisting students in expanding theirs. Education is seen as involving not only intellectual growth, but the balanced, holistic development of all potentials: feelings, mind/body integration, communication, problem-solving, dream awareness, and political and social awareness. The revolution brings with it a fresh context for education.

A context is a set of attitudes that permeates whatever

we do. It is the underlying intention that weaves together the integrity of a pattern. As teachers, we need a new context. We are no longer confident that the old context adequately meets our students' needs as whole persons. This book is concerned with a context that endeavors to take seriously one of the earliest educational ideals: Know thyself. The new context is grounded in the human drive to become all that we can become, and to go further than we have gone before.

WHAT IS CENTERING?

Centering is the term that best describes for me our experiments in self-knowledge. I first saw the idea of centering used by potters. In order to center the clay for the balanced creation of the pot, the potter must be centered within. The inner quality of centeredness is immediately manifested in the harmony of the pot. Here, I thought, is an exquisite parallel between the craft of pottery and life. Centering became for me a metaphor for living at its finest.

When I studied the martial art of *aikido,* my teacher used the term *centering* to indicate where the student's consciousness was to be placed during the practice. Ideally, we were to maintain a balanced, unified sense of ourselves while the practice unfolded. The goal was to carry a sense of loving connectedness to ourselves, others, and the universe itself during the fast and furious activity of the practice. The art was learning to encounter even an extreme adversary (such as a 200-pound attacker rushing at you!) without losing the sense of centeredness.

In the mid-seventies a personal experience led me to a deeper understanding of centering, teaching, and life. I had been propelled by a desire to know answers to these important questions: What is it that makes life seem so complicated? What can we do differently to bring about peace and harmony in our lives? What causes genuine transformation in the individual, society, and the universe? The questions led me to teachers, books, lectures, and ultimately to a Ph.D.; but I still did not learn the answers.

One glorious autumn day I was walking alone in a mountain forest. It occurred to me that I had been seeking the answers to those questions outside of myself by reading books and asking professors. I had not turned the questions over to my own experiences. I paused under a towering evergreen and simply put the questions to myself. Within seconds I was rocked by the answers; they came to me as electric rushes of energy through my entire being. When the rushes subsided I realized that the disunity between our minds and bodies makes living complicated. When we are out of harmony with ourselves, when we have feelings and needs (such as "I'm scared" or "I want recognition") but do not acknowledge these in the mind ("Big boys don't get scared" or "Don't be a show-off"), we lose touch with ourselves. Further disharmony ensues when we forget to love ourselves, and when we forget that we are connected to others and the universe. The solution is to experience ourselves deeply, love ourselves, and perceive our oneness. Each act of doing so brings us a deeper sense of unity in ourselves and a greater feeling of connectedness to all of life.

At its best, teaching, like life, is a process of learning more about ourselves and sharing that expanded wholeness with students so that they may become more unified. It is a process of finding out who we really are so that we can grant the space to others to find themselves. It is, in a word, the art of centering.

WHAT DOES CENTERING MEAN
TO THE TEACHER?

Centering is an open-ended process with an ever-expanding range of attitudes and activities. From my own experience, and from discussions with hundreds of teachers, counselors, and administrators over the past decade, I believe there are several key processes which can transform teaching into a process of centering.

These processes begin with what I call the Five Commitments:

1. A commitment to the full development of consciousness
2. A commitment to open communication
3. A commitment to learning to love ourselves and others
4. A commitment to the full development of students' potentials
5. A commitment to a world that works

Commitment One
A COMMITMENT TO THE FULL
DEVELOPMENT OF
CONSCIOUSNESS

When we commit ourselves to the full development of consciousness, our own and others, we take a profound step. We might regard this willingness to become all that we can become as the most important commitment we can make. It is important because it extends into every area of our lives.

Learning to Be Aware
This commitment means that we are willing to examine all our values, beliefs, and past actions to see if they

6

best serve our overall development. To commit ourselves to the full development of consciousness means to assume a fresh purpose. Life is no longer about survival, attainment, upholding the past, or any other previously held purposes. The commitment is simply to be everything we can be, based on an assumption that there is no limit to the human potential.

I see two components to my own education. The first component was my twenty-year long formal education from first grade through a Ph.D., which took me from Florida, my birthplace, to New England, and finally to California. The second component to my education was informal and consisted of my attempts to learn about life: how to love, deal with my feelings, to communicate, and how to solve problems. This education has taken me around the world.

The most productive phase of my informal education began in the late sixties and continues, accelerating, into the present. During this period certain key moments transformed everything. One such moment occurred in 1971 in San Francisco at a talk given by Krishnamurti, the Indian teacher and philosopher. Although I had read many of his books, his presence affected me as no book had ever done. He sat on the stage of the Masonic Auditorium, and in his calm, austere way, simply told the truth about life. He said that much of the unhappiness we experience in life, and much of the division between people and countries, is the result of our beliefs about ourselves and the world. He said that beliefs are rooted in fear, and that to be free we must let go of our beliefs and deal directly with the fear. We must see it clearly, find out about it, and let it dissolve.

The impact of that talk on me was enormous. I realized that my life was dominated by beliefs about myself, other people, and the whole world. I understood how one or two small beliefs (like "There's no way I'll ever get what I want in life" or "The world is a scary place") could influence the whole of one's life. During Krishnamurti's talk I saw that the impenetrable wall of my beliefs was actually transparent since it existed only in my mind, and for a moment I stepped through that wall. On the other side was a new world. I felt free and totally alive; I could make my life anything I wanted. Freedom was not an ideal; it was real. I could feel and breathe it.

I do not mean to suggest that my wall of beliefs was permanently dissolved. Krishnamurti cautioned us that a talk could only open the crack; the total dissolution of our beliefs would come only if we were willing to observe our moment-to-moment experiences in life.

Once I saw the garden on the other side of the wall, and that the wall existed only in my mind, I was never again able to take my beliefs seriously enough to let them limit me as they had in the past.

An advantage of a commitment to the development of consciousness is the belief that we are open to finding out the truth about ourselves and the world. Rather than blindly accepting the values and beliefs of others, we take on the responsibility of finding out the truth for ourselves. With this responsibility comes great freedom.

A second advantage is energy in growth; so to open ourselves to growth is to ensure a boundless supply of energy for ourselves. When we are closed to the full development of consciousness, it is as if we have one foot on the brakes and one on the accelerator. Life becomes tiresome and jerky. When we say "Yes!" to the full development of our consciousness, we take the brake off and roll freely. At first this may be frightening; later it is exhilarating.

A commitment to consciousness means that we are open to awareness rather than defensive of it. Much energy is wasted through resisting that which is clear for us to see should we risk opening our eyes. We are all in the process of learning about ourselves and the world around us and lessons come at us from all directions. If we resist them they seem to return even more insistently. For example, if I need to learn the lesson "Wear warm clothes on cold days," my first resistance may only cost me some shivers. If I continue to resist the lesson I might spend a few days in bed with a cold.

Learning to Feel

When we commit ourselves to developing our consciousness, we also make a commitment to understanding our feelings and learning how to benefit from them. Much of our early training takes us away from a good relationship with our feelings by teaching us perhaps to deny, ignore, or repress our feelings. If we are to develop our full potential as humans we must come into harmony with our feelings, seeing them not as aspects of ourselves to eradicate, but as good friends that can help us understand ourselves and the world around us.

Anger, fear, and sadness are feelings which we often combat. We waste energy by resisting these feelings, trying to make them go away, or ignoring them. Yet if we acknowledge these feelings and approach them with an attitude of understanding and acceptance, they can give us valuable information about ourselves. Anger, for example, can tell us when we want something but are not getting it. Fear tells us that we are in a situation which we do not have a way of handling. Sadness is a cue that something has happened to hurt us or cause us to feel loss. Feelings bring something to our attention or, in the case of fear, provide us with energy to solve a problem. So, if we are receptive to our feelings and perceive their messages, we can gain valuable information on relating to the world.

However, if we resist feelings we lose the message they attempt to bring, and experience the tension and eventual bitterness that comes from avoiding them.

Becoming Free of the Limitations of the Past

A third aspect of a commitment to the full development of our consciousness is that we rid ourselves of the limitations of the past. The belief system that enabled us to relate to our family in growing up, for example, becomes the obstacle we must overcome later. If I learned in my childhood that "Big boys don't cry," and continued to honor that belief in adult life, it could limit my access to the complete range of emotions I need to be fully human.

As we grow up, painful life experiences can cause us to make decisions about ourselves and the world. Also, our families, teachers, and others can unconsciously pass along beliefs to us that later cause us problems.

Examples of these problematic beliefs are

- I'm no good.
- If I let myself feel my feelings, the pain will overwhelm me.
- Feeling good is wrong (suffering is the natural human state).
- Being the real me doesn't work.
- I can't think.
- If I get close to people they'll hurt me.

Part of centering is spotting and letting go of limiting beliefs. As centering teachers, we need to free ourselves of limiting beliefs and assist students in doing the same.

Learning That We Are One

As our consciousness develops we begin to see that we are not only one with ourselves (our feelings, minds, and bodies) but we are also one with everything in the universe. So many of our problems as humans come from trying to disown some part of ourselves such as negative feelings. To pretend that we are not one with all aspects of ourselves is to invite a feeling of disunity and estrangement from ourselves. To deny that we are one with all else in life is to invite the alienation that some feel to be endemic to our times.

The antidote to those feelings of personal, interpersonal, and cosmic alienation is to begin to see the wholeness of all life. Of course it is easier to feel oneness with some parts of life than with others. We may readily feel it with a sunset but balk at accepting our oneness with anger, suffering, or someone we dislike. Much time and work is necessary for us to feel totally connected to ourselves, others, and the universe. The ultimate benefit of such work, however, is immense: a feeling of wholeness within ourselves and a deep resonance with the world around us.

A commitment to the full development of consciousness enables us to see the human potential from a fresh perspective.

A FRESH VIEW OF THE HUMAN POTENTIAL

Coming Back to One

Early in life we have an ability to experience ourselves deeply and express our needs directly. Then the socialization process takes over, and we are forced to leave ourselves behind and find ways to meet needs that are accepted in the particular family and society in which we live. We form a personality to help us meet our needs. The Latin root of the term *personality* is *persona,* which means mask. So our personality can be seen as a set of masks we use to get various people to recognize us. Unfortunately, these masks obscure our real personality, the person we are inside. The masks that we put on become what I think of as Personality Two. Here are some characteristics of the real us (Personality One) and the assumed us (Personality Two).

Personality One	Personality Two
feels lovable	feels unlovable, must strive for love
relaxed	tense
trusting	suspicious
feels connected to self, others, the universe	feels alienated
flexible	rigid
interested	bored
resonant to needs and feelings of others	overlooks deeper issues
communicates clearly	communicates via "games"
thinks positively	thinks negatively
gives and receives love freely	resists love
open to understanding feelings and needs	resists feelings

We have developed Personality Two to survive in an unfamiliar and sometimes hostile environment. Growth is a process of noticing when we are in Personality Two, letting it go when it no longer works for us, and finding the real us inside. It is important that we avoid the trap of thinking Two is "bad" or "wrong." The tendency to label things as bad or wrong is part of Personality Two. When we are enmeshed in Two (which is much of the time), we are simply doing what we feel we have to do in order to survive and be loved. We adopted Two when One did not work in the family, school, or society, and because we could not handle the power and intensity of One.

What Supports Personality Two?

The aspects that support Personality Two are limiting beliefs and unfelt feelings, unmet needs, mixed motives, and unseen wisdom. By observing and dealing with these aspects, we cross the bridges that lead us back to One.

Beliefs and Feelings

Feelings and beliefs go hand in hand. We have many feelings (fear, anger, sadness, sexuality) that we cannot handle, either because the feelings themselves are intense and frightening, or because we have heard some message that told us that the feelings should be repressed. One way of keeping a feeling beneath the level of consciousness is to establish a belief. For example, a young man who was abruptly abandoned by his mother early in his life had deep feelings about the event. He was scared (Who is going to take care of me?), angry (I want her back!), and sad (I miss the warmth and contact). Since he had no way of knowing how to deal with these feelings, his mind took over the job and formed some beliefs to protect him. These were beliefs like:

- Women cannot be trusted.
- Don't let anyone get too close or they'll leave you.
- People will run out on you when you most need them.

Beliefs like these can have profound effects on our lives. By the time he was thirty, this man had accrued a string of unsatisfying relationships that were characterized by rejection and lack of trust. He first presented his problem to his counselor as "bad luck with women" and "karma." As he began to see the connection between his beliefs and the events with women, he could see that luck played little part in it. He then could begin to take responsibility for his relationships with women.

Responsibility is a tricky concept to understand. Our tendency is often to equate responsibility with blame or fault. However, true responsibility is the ability to see the relationship between events. This type of responsibility has nothing to do with guilt, blame, or fault; in fact, these latter concepts keep us from taking responsibility. If being responsible means making ourselves wrong, feeling guilty, or blaming ourselves, no wonder we want little to do with it. One of the arts of good teaching is helping people take responsibility (see the connections between their beliefs and feelings and what subsequently happens to them), without thinking there is anything wrong with themselves.

Nearly any problem can be approached by looking for the limiting beliefs that support it. In the same vein, problems can be approached by looking for the feelings associated with the problem that have not been acknowledged and accepted. Because problems tend to recycle until we reach a connection with the feelings beneath them, they sometimes seem unsolvable. Problems carry a charge of emotion that must be dealt with before a rational solution can be generated. My rule of thumb is to deal with feelings first. Often, when the feelings are acknowledged and experienced deeply, the problem will dissolve naturally.

Unmet Needs

We remain enmeshed in Personality Two until we have found out the real need we are trying to meet in a given situation. In essence, a situation becomes problematic when we try to meet a need in a roundabout way.

Some of our basic needs are:

- physical (food, drink, warmth, sex)
- strokes (interactions, either positive or negative, in which we feel recognized)
- love
- feelings of self-worth or adequacy
- personal growth (getting free of old, limiting patterns and using more of our potential)
- transcendence (a sense of contact with something larger than ourselves)

It would be ideal if we learned how to spot what we need and go about meeting those needs directly. That is not the way it works on our particular planet, though. Rather, we tend to create problems as crude attempts to call attention to our needs. We can regard problems as symbolic statements of needs we are not meeting in a straightforward way. For example, a delinquent's Personality Two gets him in trouble with policemen, judges, and probation officers. If Personality One were running the show, the delinquent would see that he needs strokes from male authority figures, and he would meet that need in a way that yielded positive consequences.

I have found that seeing problems in this way opens up the possibility of solutions. The questions can then become:

- Underneath this troublesome, negative behavior, what does this person really need? What is he hungering for?
- Can he acknowledge this need?
- How can this need be met in such a way that it brings about positive consequences for himself and others?

Mixed Motives

Many of our problems come from mixed motives. Sorting out our motives and acknowledging them brings satisfaction. Our motives are mixed when we have two or more motives operating which we do not fully acknowledge.

For example, while some of us may buy a car purely for mobility, others may buy a car which projects a certain image. One of our motives may be transportation, but the other one may be to enhance our sense of self or to make us more attractive. Both of these are fine motives, but if one of them remains hidden, then a problem arises: We will never be quite satisfied with the car (we are placing a hidden expectation on it) and we will be no closer to finding a true way to enhance our self-esteem. Naturally, self-esteem must be encountered openly to be permanently enhanced. If we try to enhance it covertly, through buying things, the result may be more possessions, but not necessarily better feelings about ourselves.

A second example comes from one of my students, a woman in her thirties who returned to college to complete her education. She said that she asked her psychology instructor many questions, but never seemed to receive satisfying answers. When we discussed the situation, it became obvious that she was seeking approval from a father figure in addition to answers. The motivation was logical since she had received little approval from her own father when she really wanted it. Obviously, she also wanted answers, but the unseen motive seemed to be the one that generated the dissatisfaction. She decided to try a very creative strategy. She went directly to the instructor and asked him for some positive feedback about her work. She received some excellent compliments, and, as if by magic, she started getting better answers to her academic questions.

The Wisdom of the Current Situation

Often when we are stuck in some difficult life situation from which we would dearly like to be free, the "stuckness" has a purpose. It gives us the opportunity to gain some otherwise inaccessible wisdom. If we look upon life as a set of opportunities to learn key lessons about ourselves and the universe, we can see that each life situation, no matter how trivial or awesome, contains within it a set of lessons to be mastered. If we do not get the wisdom from the situation, we may have to repeat the lesson by creating another opportunity later. In this way, our life view is more positive. The alternatives are to see life as a set of hassles to be tolerated or as a random set of occurrences beyond our control.

The Force

The more I look inside myself and the more I work with people, the more I become convinced that we have one motivating force: the drive to experience and express pure love. When we are not able to love ourselves, and when we seek love outside ourselves in roundabout ways, we are dissatisfied because we are resisting a very powerful force. When we can open up to loving ourselves, and express our love directly to others and the universe, our lives can become richly satisfying. This is because we are open to the force of love and to letting it suffuse all of our lives. One of the best statements about the grandeur and pervasiveness of love was made by Albert Einstein, who was once asked to define space. "Space," he said, "is love." In the final analysis, when we sit down with a class or turn to face ourselves, we are looking for parts of ourselves and others that have not been loved yet.

Commitment Two

**A COMMITMENT TO OPEN
COMMUNICATION**

As our consciousness develops, several other commitments naturally emerge. Particularly important in the process of centering is learning how to communicate about ourselves openly with others, and learning how to listen to the communications of the people in our lives.

The difficulty in learning how to communicate about ourselves is that we have to overcome past failures of communication. As a result of these failures, we make decisions to shut down and keep our experience to ourselves. Unfortunately, although these decisions may work temporarily, they can eventually cause problems. Since sharing inner experiences brings people closer to one another, we must risk sharing ourselves to achieve genuinely close relationships. I have observed many teachers who were willing to be real with their students, and I have also seen many who were not. The difference this attitude makes in a classroom is awesome. Where teachers are willing to share themselves and reveal their positive and negative thoughts and feelings to their students, a feeling of lightness and freedom pervades the atmosphere. Where teachers are not willing to be real with students, where the facade is maintained at all costs, I felt a heavy and restricted atmosphere.

As consciousness grows we find ourselves learning to listen to people on deeper and deeper levels. We are no longer satisfied to hear only the surface level of their communication; we want to explore the more meaningful messages that lie below that layer. Early in our growth a child may ask, "What happens to kids when parents get divorced?", and we may respond with a dissertation on divorce and its outcome. Later, when we learn to listen to the communication beneath the surface, we may be able to draw the child out and find that he is worried about what might happen to him if his parents were divorced. Much of the communication we hear is superficial and disguises deeper issues. If we cannot hear the deeper level, we are doomed to remain on a surface level of relationship. When we have expanded our own consciousness enough to hear what is really being said, a world of rich relationship opens up for us.

Nobody, at least in my experiences, ever masters the art of listening. What matters is that we commit ourselves to *learning* to listen. If our intention is learning to hear what people are really saying, it will eventually provide the skills necessary to learn the art, and consequently allow us to deepen and expand our relationships with people.

Commitment Three

A COMMITMENT TO THE FULL DEVELOPMENT OF STUDENTS' POTENTIALS

One of the attitudes that turns teaching into the art of centering is a commitment to the development of the full potential of our students. When I was trained as a teacher in the late sixties my classes focused on how to present subject matter, and not on the students and what they were like. It never occurred to me, as I walked into that roomful of high school juniors that first day that these were people with feelings, emotional needs, family problems, untapped creative potential, dreams, and desires. I saw them as vessels to be filled with math, science, and grammar. I went home at the end of my first day of teaching shaken to my very soul. It was as if I had received a lifetime of lessons in human behavior in six short hours. I also had a colossal headache that I suspected might be permanent.

Looking back on that experience, I see that my rude awakening was due to being asleep to the full potential of myself and my students. Instead of taking them where they were and learning about them, I tried to come in with a basketful of knowledge with which to stuff them. They made it plain to me that first day that they had been stuffed to bursting already. When I settled down enough to figure out what was going on, I began to discover their reality. As I listened to them and tried to draw them out, a startling fact emerged—they had as much to teach me as I had to teach them. The real issues that concerned them were the same issues with which I still wrestled. They were caught between desperately needing independence and being afraid to go out in the world. They were socially inept, they could not express themselves well, and they were secretly aware of the difference between their facades and what was really going on inside them. Plus there were those pimples to contend with. It brought back painful memories of my teens, which had seemed like one long battle with fat and acne. Being with them helped me relive my adolescence and resolve some of the unfinished business from my teens that I had turned my back on. It became an opportunity for me to come to terms with some of my own loneliness and social ineptitude. Realizing all of this, and sharing it with the students, I was able to maintain some kind of sanity. In addition, we were able to strike a bargain. As long as we balanced my knowledge-stuffing with opportunities to explore what was really going on with each other, they were willing to put up with the subject matter. I won't say they were enthusiastic about it, but they learned enough to do well on the achievement tests.

Now, more than a decade after that first teaching experience, I have worked with all ages from pre-schoolers to, at the present, graduate students. My conclusion is that we must see our students and ourselves in the whole. If we focus on a narrow part of us, like the intellectual part, we will miss the physical, emotional, and spiritual parts of ourselves. And if we do not see the whole, our attempts to educate even the intellectual part will ultimately fail.

From my own experience it appears that if we do not use schooling as an opportunity for our students to explore and expand the wholeness of themselves, then we are apt to lose them. For a while it is not difficult to con an elementary student into believing that the traditional subject matter is important, secondary students can plainly see that there is a substantial gap between what is important in life and what is happening in their classrooms. Then comes the slack-jawed apathy, the dullness of eye, the guarded suspicion that one sees in many secondary classrooms.

Later in this book we will explore a new curriculum that uses the expansion of consciousness as an integral part of the daily subject matter of schooling. While such a curriculum may not be the panacea (we have had too many of those already in education), at least it will be a movement in the direction of a whole-person education.

Commitment Four
A COMMITMENT TO A WORLD
THAT WORKS

Part of the responsibility of teachers who are growing in the art of centering is to bring that expanded consciousness out into the social and political realm. Developing one's own consciousness is an important first step; the next movement is outward to engage in enlightened social action.

I do not know what form enlightened social action may take. I am not by nature political and think in terms of individual changes in consciousness. It seems to me that what we must do first is clearly define our intentions: We are committed to a world that works. As we each become more centered in that intention, the appropriate expression will manifest itself. As individuals we must find our own unique ways to make a difference. Making the world work better is a personal commitment as well as a political one. By modeling a commitment to a world that works, and by giving students permission to think along the same lines, teachers can make a crucial contribution to the transformation of society.

Commitment Five
LEARNING TO LOVE OURSELVES AND OTHERS

The ultimate commitment as teachers is learning to love and honor ourselves and others, and assisting our students in learning to love and honor themselves. Life takes on a rich meaning when it is seen as a constantly expanding series of opportunities to learn to love ourselves, and grow in love toward others. Even tragedies can then be viewed as opportunities to learn how to give and receive love.

There are many obstacles to loving ourselves. In the past it seemed conceited to feel good about yourself. Now, of course, we know that conceit is an attempt to convince the world that you are all right after you have come to feel bad about yourself. The very things we most need to love about ourselves (such as our negative feelings) are the very things we hate most. If you are feeling scared, for example, you will likely remain scared until you embrace your fear and love yourself for feeling that way.*

As humans we seem to have a Big Curriculum of lessons to learn about life. Among the highest lessons is

---

*For a deeper discussion of these and related issues, a good source will be *On Learning To Love Yourself,* to be published by Prentice-Hall, Inc., Englewood Cliffs, N.J.

learning to love. Since this lesson is so important, we may as well be honest about it and build it right into our work in teaching.

Centering in teaching is all about helping ourselves and our students clear away the barriers that keep us from expressing our love in pure, satisfying ways. As centering teachers, our responsibility is twofold. First, we must be in the process of centering ourselves, so that the teaching environment is alive with our own growth. We must then endeavor to choose curriculum activities that expand our students' abilities to become centered. A Curriculum for Consciousness, in the second part of this book, provides activities for a centering curriculum.

2

how to aviod
burnout in teaching

Over the past decade, by speaking to many teachers around
the world, I have tried to learn how successful teachers,
people who seem to really enjoy teaching, keep themselves
fresh and excited. In addition, I have experimented a great
deal in my own teaching to find ways of staying turned on
in this most demanding profession. Several suggestions
emerged from these discussions and explorations, several
suggestions, based on the experiences of many successful
teachers, about how to avoid burnout and thereby keep
teaching lively and interesting. These suggestions are a
combination of both attitudes (ways of viewing teaching)
and activities (things we can do on a daily basis).

TEACHING AS A LEARNING EXPERIENCE

As one teacher put it, "you teach best what you most need to learn." By viewing teaching as an opportunity to learn what we most need to know about ourselves and the world, we open ourselves to a vast and potentially exhilarating variety of lessons about life. What better place is there to learn about life than in the teaching environment? When we let go of our limiting view of teaching—that of filling empty vessels with knowledge—we can see that each teaching environment, whether it is a traditional classroom or a trip to the zoo, is a vibrant organism. Each is a microcosm of the whole universe where we can learn all the lessons of life.

Teaching, regardless of the students' ages, is an opportunity to help students resolve the developmental issues that confront them at their particular life stage. It is also an opportunity for us as teachers to deal with any unfinished business we might have from that particular stage. Examples of developmental issues confronting junior high students are:

- How to handle their sexual feelings.
- How to relate to their peer group while still maintaining a relationship with parents.
- How to deal with their body changes and their confusing world of inner experience.

Looking at those issues closely as adults, we might wonder if we have truly resolved them for ourselves. If we open ourselves to learning more about our own lives as our students learn to deal with life, teaching can become a shared journey of growth. On the other hand, if we stay closed—if we regard our students' journeys as something alien to ourselves or if we think of life as something we have already figured out—then it is quite possible that the teaching process will become stultifying.

As another teacher said, "Our best bet is to see the classroom as a mirror for ourselves." She meant that we can see what goes on in the teaching environment as a reflection of what is going on inside us. If we do that we feel part of the whole. The alternative is to see teaching as an adverse process, an "us versus them" arrangement rather than a shared journey. A case study will illustrate.

Mike, a teacher of English in a secondary school, had developed an adverse relationship with a sophomore named Todd. Todd was disrespectful, did not complete his assignments, and took the opposite position in practically every interaction with Mike. After bickering with Todd, making threats, and stewing for a while, Mike sought the advice of his department chairman. Mrs. Harper, after listening carefully to Mike's complaints about Todd, asked Mike to think about what part of himself Todd reflected. Mike's first reaction was to get angry, because he was firmly convinced he was "right" and Todd was "wrong." Mrs. Harper pointed out that in the real world things are usually not that simple, and that in a problem situation both parties usually have an investment. After thinking it over, Mike told Mrs. Harper that Todd mirrored the rebellious part of himself that he had squelched when he was in high school. He had opted for the other path, one of being a "good boy," but in so doing had never accepted and dealt with his rebellious side. He saw that Todd was giving him the gift, painful as it seemed, of an opportunity to embrace something he had denied in the past.

Later, as Mike talked to Todd, sharing with him what he had learned, Todd began to cry. It turned out that Todd had a great deal of anger toward his father who had left his home two years earlier. He was concerned about whether or not his father still loved him. Since he could not work this issue out with his father, he aimed his aggression at Mike.

The problem between them dissolved, leaving them both richer in understanding themselves and each other.

This case study illustrates that much forward progress can be made by viewing our students' lives as reflections of our own. While not all of our problems with students will resolve so quickly, the attitude itself provides a positive framework through which to view everything that occurs in the teaching environment.

To see teaching as a shared journey solves another problem. It is easy, if we view teaching as a one-way street, to fall into the trap of doing more than 50 percent of the work in the classroom. If we see teachers as having the answers and the students having the questions, we invite an imbalance in the relationship which can only cause a drain on teachers' energy. It is important to have a relationship with students which generates energy for all concerned, rather than drains it. A commitment to a shared journey can provide such an energy-building relationship.

COMMUNICATE OPENLY AND CLEARLY WITH STUDENTS, COLLEAGUES, AND PARENTS

Nearly all of the successful teachers I interviewed for this section of the book echoed the need for clear communication as a way of avoiding burnout. The reason for this is simple.

When we have something on our minds (such as a feeling or something we want from someone), the most efficient thing to do is to communicate about it. Communication clears the air and makes desired results more likely. If we do not communicate about it, preferably to the key party in the interaction, then we have generated a small bit of unfinished business in our lives. This is not immediately troublesome, but it may accumulate if we are not careful, and become a lifestyle for some people.

Unfinished business comes in many different forms:

- Things we have started and have not finished.
- People we like and have not told.
- People we are angry at and have not told.
- Things we want from people and have not asked for.
- Feelings we have had inside ourselves that we have not acknowledged.
- Things we are scared or hurt about and have not shared.

The result of accumulating unfinished business is that it causes us to withdraw from people.

Jon, a teacher in a special classroom for learning about disabled students, relayed an incident of unfinished business. His teammate did several things the first week of school that made him angry. Since he had not worked with her and did not know her, he ignored the feelings he was having. By Thanksgiving he found it difficult to be in the same room with her. Finally, when he found himself thinking about calling in sick one day just because he did not want to interact with her, he saw that he had a problem. He sat down with her and shared the whole story. She had also accumulated a number of negative feelings about him. When they revealed all their unfinished business, they saw that the feelings they had about each other were nearly identical. This conversation started them on the path to a good working relationship.

An important thing to realize about cleaning up unfinished business is that we have only to do it bit by bit. It is not necessary, nor possible, to do it all at once. However, each piece that is taken care of seems to give us the energy we need to clear up the next bit.

Life seems to work best when we stay current with our feelings, wants, and other communications. When this is not possible, the next best thing is to clear up the unfinished business soon after you spot it. When it accumulates you will notice certain symptoms, such as:

- Feeling little energy after work
- Avoiding certain students or colleagues
- Physical problems (tension, headaches, exhaustion, sleeplessness)
- Negative thoughts
- Acting or thinking judgmentally

When these or other symptoms appear, it can indicate that it is time to clear up unfinished business.

Here is a checklist to help recognize unfinished business.

Communication Checklist

Compliments I have not yet given

_____

_____

_____

People with whom I am angry

_____

_____

_____

Things I am angry about

_____

_____

_____

Things I want from people

_____

_____

_____

Things I have started and not finished

_____

_____

_____

Resentments

_____

Regrets

Positive feelings I have not shared

In communication, it is important to balance the negative with the positive. It is just as easy to accumulate positive unfinished business as it is to accumulate the negative and we must be vigilant about communicating both.

BUILD A DAILY CENTERING
ACTIVITY INTO YOUR LIFE

As one gifted teacher said, "If I take an hour for myself each day, I can give 23 back to others. If I don't take that hour for myself, the whole 24 are shot." This teacher had experienced the value of setting aside time each day for centering.

Whether we call it centering, meditation, or contemplation, we all seem to need time for ourselves; to go inside, to marshal our inner resources, and to rediscover and nurture our inner energy. If we lose touch with our sense of centeredness, and if we do not set aside time to cultivate that sense, then it is easy to feel scattered and harried.

Teaching is so demanding that it is doubly important to find ways of replenishing energy on a daily basis, so that some remains for the rest of our lives. Building a daily centering activity into your life will mean that you have made a major commitment to your own well-being.

Here is a list of centering activities used by a group of gifted teachers with whom I had a roundtable discussion.

1. Running
2. Yoga
3. Meditation (One teacher used a formal meditation, another simply sat with eyes closed for 15 minutes.)
4. Physical relaxation exercises (Such as the ones in the relaxation section of this book.)
5. A catnap
6. Hitting tennis balls
7. Modern dance
8. Painting
9. Prayer

Some of these activities make use of a focusing of the consciousness while others make use of a discharge of physical tension. Some are purely mental, physical, or spiritual, and others are a combination. Each person must find his or her own particular way of centering. There is no best way; only that which suits the person. What is most important is the willingness to make a regular commitment to your own well-being.

CALL IN WELL

Several teachers mentioned an interesting phenomenon. They sometimes take a day off when they are feeling good, or when they feel like they are beginning to come down with an illness. The advantage of the latter approach is that they are often able to nip a sickness in the bud before coming down with it in a full-fledged form. Most of us intuitively know that illness is caused not simply by viruses and their ilk, but also by our physical and mental state of being. In other words, if I am tired and need a couple of days rest, I may be much more susceptible to the flu than if I were rested. Further, it is socially acceptable to lie in bed with the flu for three days, but not so acceptable to lie in bed for three days to rest and reestablish contact with ourselves—in short, to get centered.

There are distinct advantages to a preventive approach. If we are able to sense that off-center feeling that tells us we are on the brink of illness, we may be able to halt the full onslaught of the illness. A personal experience may illustrate. Recently I felt the initial symptoms of a cold: scratchy throat, sniffles, an achy feeling in my body. I decided (for once!) to practice what I preach. I cancelled my appointments and stretched out on the rug in my office. For a half-hour or so I simply lay there with my eyes closed. Then an idea came to me. I reasoned that the oncoming cold was a message from my body to my mind.

On this assumption I asked my body what the message was. Immediately a message popped into my mind: slow down. A quick glance around my life told me that I was overextended; so busy that I was becoming harried. In addition I saw that I was shortcutting and in danger of doing sloppy work on a couple of projects. Okay, I thought, now that I have the message, maybe I can just slow down and not get the cold. But what about the symptoms? I could still feel them, although not quite as strongly as before. Another idea came to me. Perhaps if I stopped fighting and surrendered to them they would run through me quickly. And that is precisely what happened.

For 20 or 30 minutes I felt all the miserable symptoms of a cold: sneezy, achy, grouchy, and stuffy (sounds a bit like the Seven Dwarfs, doesn't it?). Then, as if by magic, I felt fine again. I spent an hour at my desk making a time schedule to organize things a little better, then went for a long walk.

Who knows whether I would have gone on to get a full-fledged cold? Who cares? It may have passed in an hour even without my interior work. It really does not matter, though, because I learned something valuable about my life from the experience. If what I did prevented a cold, I would do it again a dozen times.

I have recently experimented with taking an occasional day to be with me or to have some fun with a co-conspirator. Recently a colleague in my department and I called in well and spent the day on the ski slopes. We had a grand day of skiing, and in addition we probably got more high quality work done, chatting in the car and on ski lifts, than we would have if we had stayed in the office.

Sometimes retreating to contemplate life and work is the best favor we can do for ourselves and our employers. Each of us has the responsibility to see the forest as well as the trees in our work; we cannot afford to leave the big picture to others. Calling in well can be an opportunity to rise above the daily routine to get a better perspective on life and work.

TEACHING IS A SPECIAL KIND
OF BUSINESS

Teaching is an art, but it is also a business. Rosenshine and Furst, in their classic review of studies on teaching, found that successful teachers were businesslike as well as warm. The ability to handle the real-world mechanics of teaching can be a major factor in staying fresh.

First, like any business, teaching must keep the owners, the employees, and the customers happy. Since everybody owns education and nothing is going to please them, we must focus on the employees, largely teachers, and the customers.

For teachers, the business of teaching means managing the teaching environment to meet everyone's needs. It may also mean keeping an organized list of plans or devising a contract with the students to insure orderly behavior and completed assignments. It may mean honoring agreements made with the students and assuring proper follow-through. It may mean a reminder pinned to your desk to give Sally some extra strokes this week because she lost her guinea pig.

Business people always strive to make life easier for themselves and their customers. We may profitably view teaching this way, since our job involves selling the most important product on earth. We are in business to sell people on themselves and their full potential, and we must be sure that we as teachers prosper simultaneously with the growth of our students.

IN SUMMARY

To avoid burnout and to stay fresh in the teaching profession means to view ourselves as growing human beings, so that teaching becomes a shared journey with students. We must communicate clearly, take care of our own minds and bodies, and be businesslike in our work. From these suggestions, derived from talented teachers' strategies, we recognize that these tips transform not only teaching, but life itself.

3

centered discipline in the classroom

Handling discipline problems effectively is a hallmark of a successful teacher. Most teachers who burn out and leave the field do so primarily because of poor skills in classroom management. This chapter examines how successful teachers have built and maintained peaceful and positive classroom environments. Although the specific strategies apply more to elementary students, the general principles can be used with any age group.

BUILDING THE GREENHOUSE: SUGGESTIONS FOR CENTERED CLASSROOM MANAGEMENT

Clarify Your Goals

It is important for you as a teacher to know what sort of classroom you desire from your students. Often just knowing what you want will effect the changes. I suggest that you take time to state your goals like the following, which are taken from lists made by teachers in centering workshops.

- I want students to support and encourage each other.
- I want orderly movement from one activity to another.
- I want students to get attention directly rather than in response to poor behavior.
- I want everyone in the class to have a sense of belonging.
- I want everyone to respect the rights of others.

The benefit of knowing your personal goals is that you will be able to tell the students clearly the kinds of behavior that work best with you. That behavior will be easier to spot and, therefore, reinforce.

Help Students Spell Out Their Goals

Through discussion and other activities, students can be assisted to clarify what *they* want to experience in the classroom. The goals of children and teachers are often very similar, and I have seen goal clarification done with children as young as kindergarten age. A simple activity that can be used to accomplish this task is to go around a circle and have each child say one thing he or she would like to experience in the classroom. Do this often or until everyone has a clear understanding of what needs to happen for the class to work.

Build Rules Democratically

Have the class build rules for the classroom. The teachers are part of the class, too, and can suggest rules of their own. When rules are built, get agreements from everyone to honor them. These agreements can be contracts on paper, signed and dated, or they can be verbal. One useful activity to seal agreements is to have students and teachers state the agreements to each other, making eye contact. For example, each person might go through the list of agreements by saying to a partner:

- "I agree to support and encourage you and others to the best of my ability."
- "I agree to raise my hand when I need help."
- "I'm willing to ask for attention when I need it."

Many problems can be avoided by clarifying what the agreements are in the classroom, and having everyone commit themselves to those agreements.

Take plenty of time to make and seal rules and agreements. Sometimes it takes several weeks of meetings with students to get meaningful agreements. As the saying goes, an ounce of prevention is worth a pound of cure, and time spent in building a greenhouse in which to nurture positive behavior is time well spent.

Pass Out Plenty of Cues

Cues are suggestions and statements that remind students how things work in the class. The following are some cues:

- "In a little while we'll be going to the library, and let's remember that we need to do that quietly and orderly."
- "Today let's keep in mind our agreement to really support and encourage each other."
- "This week remember our agreement to raise hands when you need help."

Use Centering Activities
on a Daily Basis

Centering activities are best done as a regular daily part of classroom activities. Regular activities can help build consciousness in a smooth, steady way, and the systematic use of centering activities helps build positive discipline by laying a solid foundation of relaxation and communication skills.

You can choose the activities to deal with the changing constellation of issues that arise in the class. For example, during a time when there is a great deal of testing going on, you can use more relaxation activities. During a time of interpersonal conflicts, you may want to schedule mainly communication activities.

Develop an Interaction Style That Works

Handling interactions with students, particularly during a problem situation, is a true test of a teacher's skill. If interactions are handled productively, the lessons continued in even a two or three sentence interchange can have long-term positive benefits for students.

Consider the following interaction, taken from a real-life classroom encounter. A friend of mine, Gwen Findley, works each year to get her second-graders to learn how to solve their own problems. She tries to avoid doing the students' thinking for them. The following interaction took place midway through the year. Timmy approached Gwen as she was busy with papers at her desk.

Timmy:	Mike is reading too loud!
Gwen:	What can you do about that?
Timmy:	(pauses for thought) I could ask him to be quieter.
Gwen:	What if he won't?
Timmy:	I'll move my desk.
Gwen:	Great! I like those ideas.

It is a delicate task to teach children how to solve

their own problems, but the rewards are enormous. As Timmy masters the art of thinking up creative solutions to problems, he will become a more and more valuable person to have on the planet. Teachers like Gwen, who empower children to think and solve problems, are doing us all a service.

A workable interaction style is also helpful when you are asking students to change their behavior in some way. After a decade of consulting with teachers about behavior, I have come to believe that the simpler we can make our interactions the more powerful the change will be. The style I have been demonstrating in recent years is very simple, yet has been successful for hundreds of teachers. When a performance needs to be changed I recommend a step by step procedure.

1. Make eye contact with the student, and simultaneous touch contact with elementary students.
2. Make an "I'd like" statement like, "I'd like you to stop hitting Jimmy," or "I'd like you to return to your seat now."
3. Stay in contact until the performance has changed.
4. Thank them after the performance has changed.

If the performance is something that takes time, such as, "I'd like you to get your paper finished," I recommend two other steps.

1. Ask the student if he or she is willing to do it. ("Are you willing to finish the paper?")
2. If the student says "yes," get a time commitment. ("When will you give it to me?")

Although these steps are very simple it takes practice to learn how to do them in the heat of action.

Design a "Think-it-Over" Space in the Classroom

Students sometimes need time and space out of the flow of classroom interaction to evaluate their behavior and make redecisions—in short, to get centered. I have seen many teachers make effective use of a quiet corner or some other area in the classroom designated as a "think-it-over" space for students who are disruptive or in need of some quiet time.

Such procedures seem to work best when they are not used as punishment, (for example, "Go sit in the corner for 20 minutes for hitting Jimmy,"), but as an opportunity for the student to evaluate his or her behavior and make a decision or plan to solve the problem.

Have Plenty of Class Meetings

Class meetings are opportunities for teachers and students to discuss feelings, interaction problems, and other important communal issues. If they are handled correctly and held on a regular basis, class meetings can prevent discipline problems in the classroom.

In order to succeed, class meetings should be democratic and non-judgmental. All feelings and issues should be open for discussion, and everyone should have an opportunity to speak. Teachers must avoid moralistic lectures and criticism. The class meeting is an opportunity to air issues, not necessarily to solve them to completion, although many teachers who use class meetings regularly have found that problems are often solved just by airing them.

Class meetings can teach an important life skill. When problems arise or feelings are riled, we can sit down and talk about it. Often in problem situations we sulk, become aggressive, or use some other strategy that fails to meet our needs. Learning that we can deal with life's difficulties by discussing them is surely one of life's great lessons.

Give Rich, Frequent, Positive Messages to Students

In giving acknowledgment to other people, there is no need to be conservative. We can pass out hugs, compliments, praise, pats, strokes, and squeezes all day long and not diminish our supply one whit. In fact, the act of being positive in word and deed will bring back a rich flow in our direction as well.

People once believed that if you were too positive with others they would become lazy and self-indulgent. A steady stream of criticism was necessary to keep people motivated. Even when they did well, you had to be stingy with the praise, lest they rested on their laurels and became conceited. Now, of course, we see that those beliefs are nonsense, but the remnants of the old patterns still permeate many of our interactions with students and with ourselves.

One of the skills I recognize in successful teachers is the ability to catch students being good. When I visit classrooms that are humming with positiveness I hear statements like:

- "I really like the way you folks are working efficiently today."
- "Thank you for coming in promptly after recess."
- "Lois, I love the sparkle in your eyes today."
- "I like the way you helped Ruth with her work, Tim."

I think we all like to live in a world which has a positive atmosphere. We each are responsible to contribute to that atmosphere in our own creative ways. The true miracle of being a positive energy source is not getting back what you give, although that is true. The act of giving positive energy makes us feel good, too, so the old saying "To give is better than to receive," turns out to be truer than we ever expected if we understand it in a new way: "To give *is* to receive."

a curriculum for consciousness: 60 activities

introduction to the curriculum

In Chapter Two we saw how teaching is essentially an enlightened business.

In viewing teaching as a business we must keep the customer foremost in mind. Today it is evident that the customers are not buying the product the way they used to. Of the many reasons for this problem, the one that cannot be ignored is the deficiency of the product.

For too long we have tried to sell a curriculum that does not teach us much about ourselves. It does not help us to:

- Communicate our feelings
- Solve problems
- Listen to each other
- Love ourselves

- Relax
- Discover the wonder of our bodies
- Discern what we most deeply need
- Learn from our dreams
- Improve self-esteem

The current curriculum, which focuses on a narrow part of ourselves, no longer suffices. Our present era is one of wholeness and balance and when that is not served, we will turn away.

We need a curriculum for wholeness. Along with reading, writing, and other basics, this curriculum must also teach the wonder of us: the magnificence of clear communication, the miracle of learning to listen, the awe of discovering the world of our inner experience, and the world of dream, feeling, and energy.

In addition to twelve years of grammar, we must have a balance of communication skills in which we learn to listen, express how we feel, and know what we need. In addition to a decade's experience in mathematics, we need a decade of discovering our inner world and how to navigate it.

Extraordinary times call for extraordinary leaps of consciousness. The curriculum which follows is such a leap, and I do not expect that it will be adopted smoothly or quickly. One teacher called it the 2001 curriculum. I call it the Curriculum for Consciousness, and will be glad if it is in wide use by that magic year. In the meantime it will be a joyous occasion if these activities help any of us feel more loving and more able to share with others the vast potential that resides within us all.

Toward this end Gwen Findley and I have compiled these activities. Gwen, a gifted teacher and counselor in Colorado, tried out these activities as a teacher in her own second-grade classroom, and as a counselor in the classes of other teachers.

We hope you will use these activities to develop your own curriculum. Since they do not include all of the exercises that would teach the skills in which we are interested, please feel free to adapt them for your own needs. One recommendation we have for the use of the activities is to set aside some time each day, just as you would for math or social studies, so that activities like these will become a continuous part of the school day. We have seen the most positive changes when the curriculum has been used in a systematic way.

Although the activities were designed and tested in elementary schools, they may be used with minor changes at higher grade levels.

4

learning about feelings

Feelings are integral parts of us. Every moment we are in some state of feeling: happy, sad, scared, mad, or excited. Feelings are our immediate reaction to whatever happens at any one moment. If we lose touch with our feelings we lose our sense of aliveness and spontaneity. All too often school is a place where feelings are ignored or denied. But this does not make our students' feelings go away; it just makes them go elsewhere.

Many educators now feel that the emotional domain of human development is equal in importance to the cognitive domain that has been traditionally emphasized in education. After working with both young people and adults in education and counseling for ten years, I have personally come to feel that we must not ignore the powerful role of feelings in our lives. I have seen academically talented students (and teachers) crippled in their effectiveness because they did not know how to deal with their feelings.

We would be wise, then, to spend time each day assisting students in handling the emotional domain of life, just as we now spend time each day helping them handle grammar and arithmetic. Toward this end, Gwen and I have compiled a set of activities that are designed to give students access to the feeling level of their lives.

ACTIVITY #1

FOUR BASIC FEELINGS

OBJECTIVES

1. To accustom children to thinking of feelings in four groups: happy, sad, mad, or scared.
2. To demonstrate how many feelings are a combination of these basic feelings.
3. To introduce children to communicating about their feelings.
4. To help children begin to organize and understand their inner experiences.

MATERIALS NEEDED

Chart or chalkboard

INSTRUCTIONS

1. Have children sit in a circle.
2. With the children, think of as many different feelings as possible. Emphasize feelings instead of thoughts.
3. Organize the various feelings into the four categories mentioned above using the chart or chalkboard.

POSSIBLE TOPICS FOR DISCUSSION

1. Feelings are natural parts of us.

2. Feelings are to be learned from, not to be judged as good, bad, right, or wrong.
3. When feelings are understood, accepted, and discussed, they are easier to deal with.

HINTS
1. Children share feelings more easily if you as teacher are willing to share some of your feelings. Discuss what makes you angry, frightened, et cetera.
2. Attempt to accept all feelings the children discuss; avoid becoming judgmental.

TIME
20 minutes.

ACTIVITY #2

GETTING IN TOUCH

OBJECTIVES
1. To introduce children to experiencing their feelings at a deeper level.
2. To give children an opportunity to express feelings at a deeper level.

MATERIALS NEEDED
1. Large piece of paper (manila, drawing) 12×18.
2. A pen or pencil.
3. Crayons (optional).
4. Place for each child to sit and work.

INSTRUCTIONS
1. Begin by reviewing the four basic feelings.
2. Ask each child to relax and think about which of these feelings he or she has or is having today.

3. Have the children fold their paper in half and to put in each of the four squares one of the basic feelings.

4. After each feeling has been represented, ask the children to fold their paper to the feeling most present with them right now, and to draw a picture to represent it or the event leading to the feeling. (Allow children ample time to complete the activity.)

5. Ask those children willing to share to tell about their feelings and pictures.

POSSIBLE TOPICS FOR DISCUSSION

1. Many of us share the same feelings but for different reasons.

2. This kind of activity helps us to identify our feelings more clearly, and to make decisions about keeping or letting our feelings go.

3. We can understand each other better if we are aware of each other's feelings.

HINTS

Children will want you to tell them such things as how to fold their paper, where to write the feeling words, how big to make their pictures, or what color to use. Encourage children to make their own decisions.

TIME

30–45 minutes.

ACTIVITY #3

I FEEL . . .

OBJECTIVES

1. To facilitate a deeper understanding of one's self and feelings.

2. To encourage expression of feelings individually and in the peer group.
3. To help children integrate the importance of all feelings within themselves.

MATERIALS NEEDED
1. Paper and pencils for older children.
2. Chart or chalkboard for younger children.

INSTRUCTIONS
1. Make the following statements orally and allow children to record their answers or you record them.
   Statements:
   (a) I feel angry when. . . .
   (b) I feel sad when. . . .
   (c) I feel happy when. . . .
   (d) I feel scared when. . . .
   (e) I feel unloved when. . . .
   (f) I feel excited when. . . .
   (g) I feel important when. . . .
   (h) I feel lonely when. . . .
   (i) I feel needed when. . . .
   (j) I feel ugly when. . . .
   (k) I feel left out when. . . .
   (l) I feel glad when. . . .
   (m) I feel like crying when. . . .
   (n) I feel like hitting when. . . .
   (o) I feel like screaming when. . . .
   (p) I feel like laughing when. . . .
   (q) I feel like running when. . . .
   (r) I feel afraid when. . . .
   (s) I feel jealous when. . . .
   (t) I feel anxious when. . . .
   (u) I feel depressed when. . . .

    (v) I feel guilty when. . . .
    (w) I feel bored when. . . .
    (x) I feel loved when. . . .

2. If children are writing their feelings, allow time for sharing. This can be done in the large group or in small groups.
3. Lead group discussion as to the importance and worth of all our feelings.

POSSIBLE TOPICS FOR DISCUSSION

1. It is supportive to hear that our friends have the same concerns as we do.
2. A similar circumstance can trigger many different feelings depending on the person and his or her experiences.

HINTS

1. Primary age children cannot write their endings. They will miss the point because of energy put into correct spelling.
2. Be aware of students who do not participate.
3. Be aware of students who always have a violent or hostile response. Talk to them or refer them to their counselor.

TIME

30 minutes.

ACTIVITY #4

HOW WE EXPRESS FEELINGS

OBJECTIVES

1. To allow children the chance to discuss ways to vent feelings.
2. To accept differences in people's actions and reactions.
3. To give children the opportunity to hear alternative ways to deal with feelings.

MATERIALS NEEDED
Chalkboard.

INSTRUCTIONS
1. Have children join together in a semicircle close to the chalkboard.
2. Write each of the four basic feelings on the board, leaving a large space around each one for listings.
3. Begin by giving information about how we each have a different method of dealing with our feelings. Point out that we all react differently under the same or similar circumstances.
4. Brainstorm with the children about all the different ways we can express our feelings. Point out how two feelings can have the same response.

POSSIBLE TOPICS FOR DISCUSSION
1. We all react differently because we are all different people.
2. Acceptance of these differences can bring us closer together.
3. We usually do something physical when we have a feeling.

HINTS
1. Keep negative attitudes away from responses that appear unacceptable.
2. Use "could" instead of "should."

TIME
25 minutes.

ACTIVITY #5
BODY CLUES TO FEELINGS

OBJECTIVES
1. To give children information about how their bodies are indicators of the feelings inside them.

2. To provide an atmosphere of acceptance of these indicators as useful tools.
3. To help children integrate information concerning the wholeness of self.

MATERIALS NEEDED
None

INSTRUCTIONS
1. Ask children to find a space in the room that can be totally theirs, one that allows them to stretch in all directions without touching someone else.
2. Ask them to close their eyes and become very relaxed.
3. As children are settling down, begin talking quietly about feelings in a very positive manner. Bring to light how our bodies react when we experience our feelings. Use examples such as tears, smiles, or stomach aches.
4. Ask children to concentrate on being "sad" for a few minutes and to be aware of where they feel that sadness in their body.
5. Spend three to five minutes on each feeling, ending with "happy."
6. Go back through each of the feelings and ask each child to share the experience.

POSSIBLE TOPICS FOR DISCUSSION
1. Some feelings can bring about actual pain.
2. Our bodies could help us "know" a feeling before we act out in an unacceptable manner.

HINTS
1. Use positive encouraging statements when moving from one feeling to the next. Give children permission to be where they need to be.
2. Be willing to share your own feelings.

TIME
30–40 minutes.

AWARENESS OF OTHERS' FEELINGS

OBJECTIVES
1. To help children improve awareness of others' feelings.
2. To assist children in moving from a self-centered view of the world to an other-centered one.

MATERIALS NEEDED
None

INSTRUCTIONS
1. Sit in a circle.
2. Have children volunteer to act out a feeling without words. You may want to model one, like crossing your arms and stamping your feet to show anger.
3. The others try to guess what feeling is being acted out. The basic four can be used, as well as other feelings like frustration, confusion, boredom.

POSSIBLE TOPICS FOR DISCUSSION
1. How can knowing how people act out feelings be helpful in life?
2. How do people learn different ways of acting out feelings?

TIME
20 minutes.

ACTIVITY #7
GUESSING FEELINGS

OBJECTIVES
1. To give students practice in watching for and recognizing feelings in others.
2. To help students interact about their feelings.

MATERIALS NEEDED
Drawing materials: crayons, paper, pencils.

INSTRUCTIONS
1. Have students make drawings of children and adults experiencing different feelings. Have them write down on the back of the paper which feeling is being represented.
2. Break into partners or small groups, and have children take turns trying to guess which feelings are represented in the drawings.

POSSIBLE TOPICS FOR DISCUSSION
1. Which feelings are hardest to draw?
2. Which feelings are hardest to guess?

TIME
20 minutes.

ACTIVITY #8
THE "EYES" HAVE IT*

OBJECTIVES
1. To help children understand the importance of eye contact.

*This activity appeared in a slightly different form in *Transpersonal Communication,* by Barry K. Weinhold and Lynn C. Elliott (Englewood Cliffs, N.J.: Prentice-Hall, Inc., 1979), p. 58. Permission to reprint is gratefully acknowledged.

2. To encourage children to learn more about how they use their own eyes.
3. To participate on a one-to-one basis in an activity that will heighten awareness of self and others.

MATERIALS NEEDED
None

INSTRUCTIONS
1. Divide the class into small groups of three or four students.
2. Explain that they are going to express feelings by using only their eyes. They may not use their hands, voices, or any other part of their bodies.
3. Ask the children to look at each other and pay attention to one another's eyes.
4. Ask them to feel scared and to show their fears through their eyes, looking at the rest of the group as they do so.
5. Allow about a minute for each feeling, moving from scared to anger to sadness to happy.
6. Discuss what happened in this exercise with the entire group.

POSSIBLE TOPICS FOR DISCUSSION
1. Was it hard to use only their eyes?
2. Could they tell what others were feeling just by their eyes?

HINTS
1. Some children will want to use facial expression.
2. Discourage laughter.

TIME
20–30 minutes.

ACTIVITY #9

BODY AND WORD DISAGREEMENTS

OBJECTIVES
1. To offer information about how our words and actions often mask our feelings.
2. To give children tools which help them understand themselves and their environment.

MATERIALS NEEDED
None

INSTRUCTIONS
1. Have children gather together in a circle for a group discussion.
2. If necessary, give or model some of the following information:

POSSIBLE TOPICS FOR DISCUSSION
1. What we say and do often send out two different signals.
2. Most of the time our bodies are telling the true message.
3. Double messages are: shaking head "yes" while making a negative statement; shaking head "no" while making a positive statement; rapid movement of legs, hands, or feet; folded arms or crossed legs; a sudden change in pitch or speed of voice; no eye contact.
4. Ask children for additional ways we send double messages.
5. Discuss how we often speak before we think or before we feel.
6. Even if we are aware of two-way messages, we may not always be willing to change our behavior.
7. Self awareness is most important.

HINTS

1. Be willing to model behaviors.
2. Be willing to hear about your own double messages.
3. Do not expect rapid changes in children just because they have new information. Old habits are hard to break.

TIME

20–30 minutes.

ACTIVITY #10

WAYS I DEAL WITH FEELINGS

OBJECTIVES

1. To allow children the opportunity to explore many ways of dealing with feelings.
2. To experience a group commonality in dealing with feelings.
3. To begin a responsible decision-making process by which each child concentrates on what is best for him.

MATERIALS NEEDED

Paper and pencils for each child, and a comfortable place to write.

INSTRUCTIONS

1. Children can remain at their desks while discussing ways to deal with feelings.
2. Be sure the children understand that we all deal differently with feelings. Ask the students to think of different ways they use to deal with each of the four feelings and to write them down.
3. Make a group list by including any that class members wish to share.

4. In closing, ask the children to monitor themselves and others to see which methods seem most successful and unsuccessful.

POSSIBLE TOPICS FOR DISCUSSION
1. We often think we are dealing honestly with our feelings when we are not.
2. Our feelings are the same; the ways we deal with them differ.

HINTS
Be sure this activity is carried out in a nonthreatening and nonjudgmental manner. This is best done when you as teacher are accepting of all feelings and responses.

TIME
30 minutes.

ACTIVITY #11

NEW AND BETTER WAYS

OBJECTIVES
1. To provide children with new and different ways to get through feelings.
2. To allow children the time to discuss these new ways.
3. To offer children the opportunity to make responsible decisions concerning personal change.

MATERIALS NEEDED
None

INSTRUCTIONS
1. Join together in a circle.

2. Ask the children to remember the previous exercise and to think of those ways of dealing that seemed inappropriate or unacceptable. While they are remembering, give examples of your own responses that were not as effective as they could have been.
3. Ask the children to share their own ineffective ways as well as those they have seen in others.
4. Guide the discussion to things that seem to work better, both tried and untried.
5. Give children permission to think these alternatives through; thus children will not be stuck in a place of "what if it isn't right?"
6. Some appropriate alternatives that would be important to mention are:
   (a) Crying
   (b) Talking
   (c) Breathing
   (d) Writing down feelings
   (e) Hitting safe items (pillows, foam)
   (f) Throwing newspaper balls
7. Complete discussion by allowing children to relax and integrate all the new information they now have.

POSSIBLE TOPICS FOR DISCUSSION
1. The covering up or avoidance of feelings is ineffective.
2. Different circumstances warrant different methods.

HINTS
1. You, as a teacher, can model the kinds of behavior you want to see in students.
2. Allow students to give you feedback on your behavior.

TIME
30 minutes.

ACTIVITY #12

GUIDED FANTASY (BALLOON TRIP)

OBJECTIVES

1. To allow the imagination to become involved in more positive thinking.
2. To provide children a relaxed time for freedom of thought and experience.

MATERIALS NEEDED
None

INSTRUCTIONS

1. In a guided fantasy it is necessary for children to be in a place of relaxation and quiet. After establishing this quiet relaxed atmosphere, and being sure of no interruptions, communicate the following in your own style and in your own words.

   Imagine yourself outside on a wonderfully warm day. Everything around you is peaceful and calm. Somewhere in the distance you can hear the birds singing. As you feel the warmth of the sun on your body, a soft breeze begins to blow. Take some time now in this peaceful place to go inside yourself and explore all that is there. Lay back all the walls and barriers you have built and see what is inside. You will find your feelings there—let all those feelings come out and float around you in that nice breeze. Be sure to get out all the sad, mad, and scared feelings which dwell deep inside of you. Get all of them out, letting them move around you, knowing them all. (pause)

   After you have emptied them all into your space, a balloon comes by. Take that balloon and see how easy it would be to put something inside. Search through all your feelings moving about you, remove those you do not like, and put them into the balloon. Put in any that hinder clear thinking. You will see that they will never come out again. Look carefully now for those that like to hide and sneak up on you when you least expect it, and put them into that balloon. No matter how many or how big they are, your balloon can hold them. When you have gathered into the balloon all you want, tie the end very tightly. When you are ready, let it go—let it float up and away from you and be caught by the wind and take away all those unwanted feelings. Watch it become smaller and smaller and feel that warm breeze suddenly catching your hair and caressing your face. The balloon is just a speck now; take a good deep breath and relax in your space as the balloon is gone. Let your mind and body come together now and listen and feel all that is around you.

When you are ready, quietly return here feeling rested and full of positive energy.

End of fantasy.

2. When children seem ready, move to a quiet discussion about their experience.

3. After the discussion have a quiet reading or drawing time, or move on to exercise #13.

POSSIBLE TOPICS FOR DISCUSSION

1. The amount remembered will differ with each individual.
2. If some feelings would not stay in balloon, there must be a need to keep them.

HINTS

1. Be positive to each child's experience.
2. Next activity needs to be low-keyed.
3. No moral or lesson to be learned, only a new pleasant experience.

TIME
45–60 minutes.

ACTIVITY #13

FOLLOW-UP TO BALLOON FANTASY

OBJECTIVES
1. To give children an opportunity to wind down after fantasy.
2. To help children integrate their recent experience.
3. To alleviate any concerns about feelings that were difficult to let go.

MATERIALS NEEDED
Modeling clay for each youngster and an appropriate working area.

INSTRUCTIONS
1. Provide each child with clay.
2. Ask them to choose one of the feelings they just put into the balloon. It could be an easy or difficult one to keep or send away.
3. Ask children to let that feeling move all over them, through their hands, and into the clay.
4. Let them mold and manipulate the clay however they need to.
5. Move among the children asking them about what they are doing.
6. When activity time is over ask the children to put the clay away and move on to a new class project.

POSSIBLE TOPICS FOR DISCUSSION
1. Using the clay helped in calming children down.
2. Some feelings always seem to be around.

HINTS
1. Mold some clay yourself.
2. Some children may prefer to do nothing.
3. Be accepting and positive towards the children's needs.

TIME
20–30 minutes.

ACTIVITY #14

FEELINGS STOREHOUSE

OBJECTIVES
1. To promote processes of self-awareness. This exercise is a follow-up on the previous two.
2. To give children the chance to discover where they store feelings.

MATERIALS NEEDED
None

INSTRUCTIONS
1. Gather in a circle.
2. Ask the children to spend three to five minutes remembering the balloon fantasy and clay exercise. As they are doing this, tell them we do not always have the chance to release our feeling in a balloon. What we do instead is store them inside us somewhere.
3. Have children get in a comfortable position either closer in the circle or away from it.
4. Ask them to think of "sad" for a moment and find where they keep that feeling in their body.
5. Spend an ample, comfortable amount of time (maybe two or three minutes) on each of the four feelings.

6. When all feelings have been spoken, allow time with the children to share where they store their feelings.
7. Close with words about how this information can be beneficial to us in understanding ourselves.

POSSIBLE TOPICS FOR DISCUSSION
1. Sometimes we store feelings without knowing it (by habit). (Girls sometimes store mad feelings, while boys store their "scared" feelings.)
2. It is okay to store feelings if we keep our warehouse clean and uncluttered.
3. Adults store feelings too.
4. Sometimes we actually hurt in our storing place.

HINTS
Be willing to share yourself.

TIME
30 minutes.

ACTIVITY #15

GRIPE TIME

OBJECTIVES
1. To allow children the opportunity to voice negative opinions about things.
2. To hear that others have the same concerns.
3. To discuss with the children that it is okay not to like everything.

MATERIALS NEEDED
Chart or chalkboard; paper and pencils for each child.

INSTRUCTIONS

1. Using chart or chalkboard, write the following:
   (a) What bothers you at home?
   (b) What bothers you at school?
   (c) What bothers you in the world?
   (d) What bothers you about your friends?
   (e) What bothers you about yourself?
2. Ask children to think about each topic.
3. Have children list entries under any or all of the topics. Younger children may need to make a group list on the board.
4. When children seem finished, open up the topics for sharing.
5. When sharing is over, ask the children how the gripe time has helped them.

POSSIBLE TOPICS FOR DISCUSSION

1. This kind of activity acts as a release, allows for disclosure, and makes gripes seem easier to handle.
2. Children may view their lives differently after activity.

HINTS

1. Be open to hearing gripes about school.
2. Give suggestions such as family, hairstyle, or oil crisis if the children seem stuck. Do not give them all their answers.
3. Make a list yourself.

TIME

20–30 minutes.

WHAT COLOR IS A FEELING?

OBJECTIVES
1. To use art as a medium to better understand feelings.
2. To provide an environment of safety to express feelings.

MATERIALS NEEDED
1. Use of any medium involving color would be suitable (tempera, watercolor, finger paint).
2. Paper appropriate to the medium chosen.
3. Suitable working area.

INSTRUCTIONS
1. Ask each child to choose a feeling close to him right now and also one color that represents that feeling.
2. Using the medium chosen, draw a picture.
3. Ask children individually or as a group why they chose that color and to tell about the picture.

POSSIBLE TOPICS FOR DISCUSSION
1. Sometimes colors can elicit a feeling.
2. Certain colors are associated with certain feelings.

HINTS
1. Show children how colors can be shaded to produce desired effects.
2. Avoid using descriptive words when referring to color because they might stereotype a certain feeling, such as "dark" blue or "bright" orange.

TIME
Up to one hour, depending on working area.

ACTIVITY #17

HOW DOES A FEELING SOUND?*

OBJECTIVES
1. To offer children a larger frame of reference when working with feelings.
2. To work in a group developing a presentation.
3. To begin developing an awareness as to the importance of feelings.

MATERIALS NEEDED
None

INSTRUCTIONS
1. Divide class into four groups.
2. Have each group work with one of the four basic feelings, which you can either assign or have the groups select.
3. Tell each group to think of up to ten ways their feeling sounds and to decide how they can present this to the class (individually or as a group).
4. Each group then makes its presentation using only sounds—no words or movement.
5. After each group, discuss which of these sounds were true or not for the rest of the class.

POSSIBLE TOPICS FOR DISCUSSION
1. Some feelings have the same sound.
2. Sometimes it is helpful to make these sounds when we are having a feeling.

*This activity appeared in a slightly different form in *The Second Centering Book*, by Gay Hendricks and Thomas B. Roberts (Englewood Cliffs, N.J.: Prentice-Hall, Inc., 1977), p. 140.

HINTS
1. Give positive feedback as to the way the groups worked together.
2. Be sure you are in an area where loud noises are acceptable.

TIME
30 minutes.

ACTIVITY #18

I FEEL . . . BECAUSE I . . .

OBJECTIVES
1. To help children own their feelings.
2. To encourage children to be responsible for themselves.
3. To reinforce decision-making processes in children.

MATERIALS NEEDED
Paper and pencil for each child.

INSTRUCTIONS
1. Ask children to complete the following statements five different ways:
   - (a) I feel happy because I. . .
   - (b) I feel angry because I. . .
   - (c) I feel sad because I. . .
   - (d) I feel mad because I. . .
2. Have a group discussion about how it is easy to blame others for our feelings. Talk about what was easy or hard to complete.

POSSIBLE TOPICS FOR DISCUSSION
1. How could this be beneficial to them in the future?
2. How important is the word "I"?

HINTS

1. Children will want to eliminate the second "I" in the statement.
2. Do the activity yourself and share with the class.

TIME

30 minutes.

ACTIVITY #19

HOW DO YOU FEEL NOW ABOUT FEELINGS?

OBJECTIVES

1. To allow children to examine the growth of their awareness about feelings.
2. To reaffirm the worth of experiencing feelings deeply.

MATERIALS NEEDED

Paper and pencil

INSTRUCTIONS

1. Join together in a circle for discussion.
2. Ask children to remember back to when they first started working with feelings.
3. Provide time for sharing.
4. Ask them to take a little trip in their minds through the times you have spent together learning about feelings and up to the present.
5. Ask the children to think of the changes that have occurred in their lives.
6. When they feel comfortable in doing so, have them return to their seats and complete this sentence. "I was _____ and now I am _____."

74

7. Allow the children to share the sentences with the group if they choose to do so.

POSSIBLE TOPICS FOR DISCUSSION
1. Some children may not experience any differences.
2. Children could follow up with what they like and dislike about their changes.
3. Whatever has occurred in the children's lives is good, important, and necessary.

HINTS
1. These are excellent statements of positive reinforcement for children.
2. Do a self-inventory and evaluation.

TIME
30–40 minutes.

5

communication skills

Communication is the thing that humans do best, and worst. We can use the power of words to help us put a spaceship on the moon, but we can get so lost in the middle of words that we cannot communicate how we feel or what we need to people close to us. In the building of a curriculum for consciousness we must include a great deal of practice in communicating effectively with each other. Practice is really all it takes. The rules of good communication are simple and straightforward, but it takes practice to remember them in the heat of action. I would like to see students leave high school with twelve years' daily experience in communication and problem-solving, just as they now leave with twelve years' experience in grammar. Few people get in serious trouble in life because of bad grammar; many people are in trouble because they cannot communicate with themselves and each other.

The following activities are designed to teach basic rules of clear communication. They are also fun, if the reactions of the teachers and students who tested them are an accurate reflection. Try these activities, add some of your own, and, if you have an extra moment, drop us a note to let us know some of your results.

ACTIVITY #1

LEARNING ABOUT A NEIGHBOR

OBJECTIVES

1. To ease tensions in a new group situation.
2. To allow children to talk to one another.
3. To help with the introductions of the class.

MATERIALS NEEDED

None

INSTRUCTIONS

1. Ask children to choose a partner, preferably someone they do not know.
2. Tell them to find out all they can about each other, because they are going to introduce each other to the rest of the class.
3. Have each child introduce his or her new friend.
4. Allow children to correct each other or make additions if they so choose.
5. Encourage and praise each child for his or her information.

POSSIBLE TOPICS FOR DISCUSSION

Ask children which was harder: to talk about themselves or someone they did not know.

HINTS
1. Join in the activity, serving as a good model for the class.
2. Tell children they could include such things as name, address, age, number of brothers and sisters, or likes and dislikes.

TIME
30 minutes.

ACTIVITY #2

GUIDELINES FOR GOOD COMMUNICATION

OBJECTIVES
1. To provide unity in methods of communication.
2. To teach basic rules of clear communication.

INSTRUCTIONS
1. Conduct a discussion covering the following points:
   (a) Avoid ignoring or belittling each other. Focus on positive ("put-ups") rather than the negative ("put-downs").
   (b) Speak for yourself, using an "I" point of view. ("I like cats" rather than "People like cats.")
   (c) Avoid interrupting others while they are talking.
   (d) Listen carefully to what others are saying.
2. Ask students for some rules of good communication that the class could adopt.

POSSIBLE TOPICS FOR DISCUSSION
1. How can you tell somebody, in a helpful way, that his or her behavior is bothering you?
2. How can we make sure we follow these guidelines?

TIME
30 minutes.

ACTIVITY #3
INTRODUCING SELF

OBJECTIVES
1. To give students practice in using "I" statements.
2. To give children practice speaking to others on a personal level.
3. To begin to develop listening skills.

MATERIALS NEEDED
None

INSTRUCTIONS
1. Divide the class into groups of four or five people.
2. Let each person in the group spend two minutes talking about himself using "I" statements.
3. Walk around the classroom keeping track of time and making sure all children take their turns.
4. After each person's sharing time, the group may want to ask follow-up questions.
5. The entire group can join together and discuss the use of "I" statements.

POSSIBLE TOPICS FOR DISCUSSION
It is easier to keep track of what a person is saying when he or she communicates openly.

HINTS
Children will benefit from your serving as a model.

TIME
    30–40 minutes.

ACTIVITY #4

I LIKE . . .

OBJECTIVES
    1. To offer children unconditional acceptance of their likes.
    2. To use "I" statements at a more personal level.
    3. To allow children to hear and integrate what they like.

MATERIALS NEEDED
    None

INSTRUCTIONS
    1. Have each child choose a partner.
    2. Each pair needs to find a quiet place to sit close together for talking.
    3. Have the children decide who will be the talker first and who will be the listener. Explain that each person will have a turn.
    4. Tell children to spend five minutes telling their partners all the things they like about themselves, their family, and so on.
    5. The partner is to only listen and not respond in any way.
    6. After five minutes have children change roles.
    7. Join back together as a group and discuss what it was like to say all our likes without having them questioned.

POSSIBLE TOPICS FOR DISCUSSION
    1. It feels awkward to do this exercise.
    2. Others' topics aroused new ones in self.
    3. It is a good feeling to be accepted unconditionally.

HINTS

Time to think is allowed, unless it is an avoidance of the task.

TIME

25 minutes.

ACTIVITY #5

I DISLIKE . . .

OBJECTIVES

1. To offer children unconditional acceptances of their dislikes.
2. Use of "I" statements.
3. To allow children to hear and integrate what they dislike.

MATERIALS NEEDED

None

INSTRUCTIONS

Same as Activity #4, replacing likes with dislikes.

POSSIBLE TOPICS FOR DISCUSSION

1. Was this exercise more difficult than Activity #4?
2. Discussion Topics 2 and 3 from activity #4.

HINTS

1. This exercise may be more difficult.
2. Dislikes are not readily accepted in our society.

TIME

25 minutes.

ACTIVITY #6
BODY LANGUAGE

OBJECTIVES

1. To inform students how we use our bodies as well as our words to communicate.
2. To give children the opportunity to communicate with their bodies.
3. To offer time to consider how body language is used constantly by everyone.

MATERIALS NEEDED

A place large enough for gross motor movement, and suitable for making loud noises.

INSTRUCTIONS

1. Tell the children that you are going to ask them to communicate some different feelings. They are to use only their bodies, not words (moaning, crying, screaming are acceptable), and they may not touch anyone else.
2. Go through each of the basic four feelings (happy, sad, mad, afraid) and combinations of these, allowing children to demonstrate each one.
3. Bring the group together and discuss the little things people do to communicate to us (tapping toes, driving fast).
4. Have children monitor themselves and others for the next few days and then move on to the next exercise.

POSSIBLE TOPICS FOR DISCUSSION

1. Some people do very small things with their bodies (twitching, tense jaw).
2. Sometimes it is difficult to communicate a feeling.

HINTS

1. Some children may find it difficult to be physically demonstrative.
2. Some children will stray from the task of communicating to being noisy. This may be an appropriate outlet for them.

TIME

30 minutes.

SHARING PERCEPTIONS

OBJECTIVES

1. To give children the opportunity for deeper self-awareness.
2. To offer children the experience of being more aware of others.

MATERIALS NEEDED

None

INSTRUCTIONS

1. Join the group together in a circle for a discussion.
2. Discuss how you demonstrate feelings in your body action, and how you have seen others do the same.
3. Encourage children to do the same kind of sharing about themselves and others.
4. Allow the children to decide which of these actions are things they would like to do.
5. Relax together and let this information be processed by all.
6. Tell children this information can be very important to them in terms of how they deal with their own feelings.

POSSIBLE TOPICS FOR DISCUSSION

1. Some ways to deal with feelings are acceptable and some are not.
2. What ways work best for you?
3. Some adults do not seem to do anything about their feelings.

HINTS

1. Do not assume a judgmental position about how children or members of their family deal with feelings.
2. Be positive in helping children look at alternatives.

TIME

30 minutes.

ACTIVITY #8

NO TALKING ALLOWED

OBJECTIVES

1. To give children a deeper look at communication through behavior.
2. To emphasize how things are different than they appear.

MATERIALS NEEDED

Paper and pencil, a place to write.

INSTRUCTIONS

1. Ask children to think of a time when their feelings were misunderstood by someone else.
2. Ask them to relax and think about that time for a few minutes.
3. It might be good to divide into small groups at this time.
4. One child at a time will demonstrate and communicate

this misunderstood feeling with only his feet. All others will write down what that communication meant to them.

5. Continue moving up the body to the legs, torso, arms, and finally the face.
6. Ask children to discuss what differences they saw in the body movements and how this could be deceiving at one time or another.
7. Continue the activity until all children that wanted to have participated.
8. Follow up closely with Activity #9.

POSSIBLE TOPICS FOR DISCUSSION

1. Sometimes our feelings are confused and therefore our communications are also.
2. The same type of movement could mean different things to different people.

HINTS

If the following is not done, do something to use the class energy in a positive way (singing, outdoor walking or playing, drawing).

TIME

30 minutes.

ACTIVITY #9

WORDS, WORDS, WORDS

OBJECTIVES

1. To provide children with a release mechanism from previous exercise.
2. To give children a quiet time to be introspective.
3. To give children an opportunity to take care of old feelings.

MATERIALS NEEDED

Scissors, glue, newspaper, one piece of construction paper.

INSTRUCTIONS

1. Give each child several pages from a newspaper, and the other materials listed.
2. Tell children to search through the pages of a newspaper for words that tell about themselves and their feeling that was the topic of Exercise #8.
3. Ask children to glue these words to their paper in any way they choose.
4. Display those of children who want theirs displayed.

POSSIBLE TOPICS FOR DISCUSSION

1. The number of words is not important.
2. This is a time to think about one's self.
3. Letters may be cut out and put together to make words that cannot be found.

HINTS

1. Some basic feeling words may need to be spelled on the chalkboard for primary children.
2. Assist children but avoid doing their thinking for them.

TIME

20–25 minutes.

ACTIVITY #10

BEHIND THE SCREEN #1

OBJECTIVES

1. To communicate with only our voices.

2. To help develop better listening skills.
3. To offer the opportunity to share a communication in a new way.

MATERIALS NEEDED
Paper and pencil. A screen of some kind to hide the communicator.

INSTRUCTIONS
1. Each willing child takes a turn behind the screen communicating to the class a feeling by voice only. Just sound, no words.
2. Each student writes down what he or she has heard.
3. Give the person behind the screen the feedback from the class.
4. Discussion may follow each communication or come at the end of the exercise.

POSSIBLE TOPICS FOR DISCUSSION
1. We all hear different things from different people.
2. There is no wrong or right answer in this exercise.

HINTS
1. Children will probably perceive correct feelings much of the time.
2. Be aware that a child unwilling to participate may need some individual attention.

TIME
20 minutes.

BEHIND THE SCREEN #2

OBJECTIVES
1. To allow children to examine their communications with themselves.
2. To give children space to verbally state how others arouse feelings.
3. To realize how we are all very individual in our perceptions.

MATERIALS NEEDED
A screen, paper, and pencils.

INSTRUCTIONS
1. Ask willing participants to think of a statement made by someone else that elicits feelings within them. This statement can stir up any one of the four basic feelings.
2. The child is to make the statement from behind the screen.
3. The class is to write down what feeling is aroused in each of them.
4. Comparisons and discussions will follow each person.
5. Ask children to communicate what they have learned from this exercise.

POSSIBLE TOPICS FOR DISCUSSION
1. How we perceive something depends on such things as our frame of mind, amount of sleep or food, or home life.
2. Some statements may have meant something completely different.

HINTS
Children will want to blame others for their feelings. Emphasize that how they feel is their decision.

TIME
    30 minutes.

ACTIVITY #12
LISTENING TO ONE ANOTHER*

OBJECTIVES
1. To teach children the difference between listening and not listening to each other.
2. To offer children the opportunity for self-analysis of listening skills.
3. To discuss a deeper awareness of the rights of self and others to be heard.

MATERIALS NEEDED
    None

INSTRUCTIONS
1. Ask for four to six volunteers to come to the front of the classroom for a discussion. Give them a topic to discuss.
2. Tell them to answer each other with statements that are not really related to what the other says. For example, one person says, "I'm going to play after school with Billy," another answers, "I have a brother named Billy," and another person says, "My brother goes to high school."
3. Have them carry this conversation on for about five minutes.
4. Ask them how they felt hearing these responses. Have they ever had this kind of conversation?

*Barry Weinhold and Lynn C. Elliott, *Transpersonal Communication: How to Establish Contact with Yourself and Others*, © 1979, pp. 54–55. Reprinted by permission of Prentice-Hall, Inc., Englewood Cliffs, N.J.

5. Ask this group to have a new conversation, this time paying close attention to what the topic is and responding only to what the person is saying. Ask them to decide if what they find important is relative to the conversation.
6. Again ask about this kind of exchange. Was it different? Which was better?

POSSIBLE TOPICS FOR DISCUSSION
1. How does it feel when someone does not listen? When this happens, what do you do?
2. Feelings are easily aroused when communications are not smooth and flowing.

HINTS
1. This can be a small group activity so everyone has an opportunity to participate. A group demonstration would be helpful.
2. Ask if everyone is willing to be sure they are listening and responding to each other.

TIME
30 minutes.

ACTIVITY #13
I LIKE YOU BECAUSE. . .

OBJECTIVES
1. To allow children the opportunity to give positive information to their peers.
2. To give children the opportunity to hear positive information about themselves.

3. To build strength in offering good information to those we care about.
4. To give children the experiences of liking themselves.

MATERIALS NEEDED
None

INSTRUCTIONS
1. Children need to have a partner and find a quiet place to share together.
2. Children should decide who will be the listener and who will be the talker first.
3. They are to tell their partner all the different things they like about him or her. The partner is to only listen and not respond.
4. After three to five minutes change roles. Time varies according to age of the group.
5. Bring the group back together and discuss the children's experiences.

POSSIBLE TOPICS FOR DISCUSSION
1. What was easiest to do?
2. What was hardest to do?
3. Include such things as discomfort, discounting, or eye contact.

HINTS
1. Laughter is a good way to avoid listening.
2. Some children will feel a need to justify such good information. Assure them that they are worthy of this positive information and to let it be a part of them.
3. Be sure children are beginning each statement with "I like you because."

TIME
    20–30 minutes.

ACTIVITY #14
I LIKE ME BECAUSE. . .

OBJECTIVES
  1. To allow children to like themselves openly.
  2. To provide a safe atmosphere for children to like them-
     selves.
  3. To develop an attitude that it is okay to like one's self.

MATERIALS NEEDED
    None

INSTRUCTIONS
  1. Ask children to choose a partner, preferably not the same
     one as in the previous exercise.
  2. Decide who will talk first and who will listen first.
  3. The children are to complete the sentence "I like me
     because. . ." to their partner. The partner is to remain
     quiet and maintain eye contact.
  4. At the end of three to five minutes change roles. Time will
     vary according to age.
  5. When all children have completed their turns, join together
     for group discussion and processing.

POSSIBLE TOPICS FOR DISCUSSION
  1. It is uncomfortable to talk about one's self in such a
     positive way.
  2. Did they say things they do not believe?
  3. How many things were original and how many came from
     other people.
  4. Eye contact is difficult to maintain.

HINTS

1. Children will be uncomfortable in this exercise. Give them permission and acceptance to be scared. Give them positive messages about doing the exercise.
2. Your modeling is an excellent way to get good individual participation.

TIME

30 minutes.

ACTIVITY #15

BOX OF GOODIES . . . (1 Item)

OBJECTIVES

1. To demonstrate how communications need to be clear and complete.
2. To give examples of how easily misunderstandings can occur.
3. To point out differences in our perceptions.

MATERIALS NEEDED

1. Paper and pencil for each child.
2. A box with a hole large enough to reach the things inside. Put one of the following in the box: candle, figurine, stuffed animal, salt shaker, chalk, fruit, and so on. Do not tell children what is in the box.

INSTRUCTIONS

1. Ask four children to be first.
2. Instruct the first child to reach in the box with one hand and to describe the first item he touches. This will keep him from feeling around.
3. The next child will do the same, but not use the same descriptive words.

4. As each takes his turn, the class will write down what they think that child was holding according to what he or she said.
5. Share with each other what the different things were.
6. This can be repeated as long as children are unaware that only one item is in the box each time.
7. After children have finished describing what they feel, reveal the items to the class.

POSSIBLE TOPICS FOR DISCUSSION
1. Partial amounts of information can lead us to misbeliefs.
2. How does this activity relate to communicating clearly?

HINTS
If children guess the item is the same, give them praise for communicating effectively.

TIME
30 minutes.

ACTIVITY #16
NOW WHAT?

OBJECTIVES
1. To allow children to integrate the information about effective communications.
2. To demonstrate to children that they are responsible for effective communication.
3. To allow processing to take place without commitment to definitive action.

MATERIALS NEEDED
None

INSTRUCTIONS
1. Join together in a circle for discussion.
2. Ask children to think about what they know concerning effective and noneffective communications.
3. Share these perceptions.
4. Ask them to think of a positive way to use this information to make their lives easier.
5. Introduce the concept of wanting and needing things into the conversation. Have children generate the correlation between wanting and needing, and effective communication.
6. End the exercise with the group relaxing and thinking about all that has been discussed.

POSSIBLE TOPICS FOR DISCUSSION
1. Asking others for what we want and need is important.
2. Effective communications help us achieve what we want and need.
3. Wants and needs are important to fulfill.

HINTS
People are guilty of thinking that another person can and should guess what they want with a minimal amount of information.

TIME
30 minutes.

ACTIVITY #17

DISCUSSION OF WANTS AND NEEDS

OBJECTIVES
1. To demonstrate the difference between wants and needs.

2. To give children permission to want and need.
3. To offer opportunity for a greater awareness of self.

MATERIALS NEEDED
Chalkboard or chart.

INSTRUCTIONS
1. Have the group generate all the things they want and need without differentiating between the two. These could be listed on the chalkboard.
2. Ask the children to consider the difference between wanting and needing. A simple definition is: wanting is luxury; needing is necessity.
3. The group can then place all the items listed in either the wants or needs category. Ask them to be realistic in their decisions (for example, nobody needs love).
4. Ask each child to relax and think of things they want or need that are or are not in the lists.
5. Close with a class discussion.

POSSIBLE TOPICS FOR DISCUSSION
1. Some things appear to fit in both categories.
2. It is okay to want and need.
3. How do we get these wants and needs?

HINTS
Some children will resist believing it is okay to need. Assure them and give them time to adopt this new attitude.

TIME
20–30 minutes.

I WANT. . .

OBJECTIVES
1. To allow children to conceptualize any and all things they want.
2. To give children permission to want unconditionally.
3. To motivate children to be aware of their wants on a deep level of awareness.

MATERIALS NEEDED
Paper and pencil.

INSTRUCTIONS
1. Depending upon the age of the group, use the following headings:
Intermediate
(a) Material
(b) Physical
(c) Emotional
(d) Mental
(e) Spiritual
Primary
(a) Things that can be touched or used.
(b) Things dealing with the body.
(c) Things dealing with the heart.
(d) Things dealing with the mind.
(e) Things dealing with good feelings.
2. Ask the children to list five to seven wants under each category.
3. Allow time for sharing by those who so choose.

POSSIBLE TOPICS FOR DISCUSSION
1. How can we get these wants from others and from our-selves?
2. Direct, effective communication is a must in getting what we want.
3. Of all these things, what one thing would you want most?

HINTS
1. Do not be judgmental about the wants of children.
2. Tell the children it is okay to want things they do not think they will ever have.

TIME
30 minutes.

ACTIVITY #19
I NEED . . .

OBJECTIVES
1. To allow children to conceptualize any and all things they need.
2. To give children permission to need unconditionally.
3. To motivate children to be clear about their needs.

MATERIALS NEEDED
Paper and pencils.

INSTRUCTIONS
1. Depending upon the age of the group, use the following headings:
Intermediate
(a) Material
(b) Physical

(c) Emotional

(d) Mental

(e) Spiritual

Primary

(a) Things that can be touched or used.

(b) Things dealing with the body.

(c) Things dealing with the heart.

(d) Things dealing with the mind.

(e) Things dealing with good feelings.

2. Ask the children to list five to seven needs under each category.

3. Allow time for sharing by those who so choose.

POSSIBLE TOPICS FOR DISCUSSION

1. How can we get these needs from others and from ourselves?

2. Direct, effective communication is a must in getting what we need.

3. Of all these things, what one thing do you need the most?

HINTS

Be nonjudgmental about needs of children.

TIME

30 minutes.

6

building responsibility

Responsibility is something that we desperately hope students will learn in school. Many do, of course, but many do not learn or accept it as well. Although many educators would agree that responsibility is a worthy goal, we seem to expect that students will learn it as a by-product of the cognitive material they are receiving. In this section we take a more straightforward approach to the teaching of responsibility. We have designed a set of activities that teach the skills of responsibility directly. By setting aside a few minutes each day for direct lessons in responsibility, we think you will see a rapid change in the level of responsible behavior in the classroom.

ACTIVITY #1

WHERE DOES IT ALL BEGIN?

OBJECTIVES
1. To develop an awareness of being responsible.
2. To introduce the class to the meaning of responsibility.

MATERIALS NEEDED
None

INSTRUCTIONS
1. Have children sit in a circle for a group discussion.
2. Introduce the concept of responsibility as "the ability to respond."
3. Ask for a discussion of the following:
   (a) Who is responsible for values?
   (b) How about school age children?
   (c) When are you responsible for yourself?
4. Ask the class to discuss these and other topics about responsibility that arise.
5. Encourage children to think and make reasonable decisions.

POSSIBLE TOPICS FOR DISCUSSION
1. Responsibility belongs to all of us.
2. Differing opinions are not necessarily right or wrong.

HINTS
Let children lead the conversation in the direction they want and need.

TIME
20 minutes.

THE COOKIE JAR

OBJECTIVES
1. To present situations in which children must make decisions about responsibility.
2. To bring about awarenesses related to their own responsibility.
3. To allow children to be responsible for making choices.

MATERIALS NEEDED
Several problem stories in which responsibility could belong to several people, such as:

(a) Mother leaves the cookie jar in an available place and the jar is broken.

(b) A fight starts over an accidental tripping.

(c) Teacher provides children with free time and one child takes advantage of it without finishing his work.

Other stories, perhaps relevant to specific classroom situations, can be used. These stories need to be presented to the group in the teacher's natural style.

INSTRUCTIONS
1. Present stories one at a time and allow for discussion after each. Allow children to disagree, but not to decide one way is wrong and one way is right.
2. Lead children to think of themselves as the main characters and to think of the decisions they would have made.

POSSIBLE TOPICS FOR DISCUSSION
1. Situations often determine the decision that is made.
2. How could a different decision affect the outcome of the story?

HINTS
1. Children like to be right. These stories have no right or wrong answers.
2. Be accepting of children and their ideas.

TIME
20–30 minutes.

ACTIVITY #3
AND THEN WHAT HAPPENED?

OBJECTIVES
1. To make a decision based on facts given about responsibility.
2. To give children permission to think for themselves.

MATERIALS NEEDED
1. Paper and pencil for older children.
2. Drawing paper for younger ones.

INSTRUCTIONS
1. Give an account of the following story or develop one of your own for which the children have to supply the ending: While Tommy and his best friend, Billy, were playing around in the classroom without permission, Billy accidentally broke a vase on the teacher's desk. Billy told Tommy that if Tommy tattled on him, he would no longer be his friend. Tommy knew that they were both in the building without permission, and he really liked Billy as a friend. Just then, they heard someone coming and both boys hurried to the playground. When they returned to the classroom, the teacher had cleaned up the mess but did

not ask any questions about what had happened. What would you do if you were: a. The teacher? b. Billy? c. Tommy?

2. Older children can write or draw how they would behave as each of these persons. Younger children would probably get better results if they drew their reactions.
3. Encourage children to share their ideas and display on the bulletin boards their pictures and stories.

POSSIBLE TOPICS FOR DISCUSSION

1. It is difficult to admit being wrong and being responsible for our own mistakes.
2. We should learn from our mistakes, not fear them.

HINTS

Some children will want to blame Billy for everything. Point out how Tommy made a decision to be in the building.

TIME

30 minutes.

ACTIVITY #4
THE TRASH BIN

OBJECTIVES

1. To free children from the habit of blaming others.
2. To use the negative energy in blaming as a catalyst to a more positive direction.
3. To give children the opportunity to share with their peers, thus gaining acceptance of themselves.

MATERIALS NEEDED
Chalkboard or chart.

INSTRUCTIONS
1. Join children together in a semicircle around a chart or the chalkboard.
2. Put at top: "People make me . . ." (Example: People make me do chores I do not like.)
3. Generate all the things you can from the class and list them on this chart.
4. Make sure each contributor uses the entire statement.
5. Close with discussion.

POSSIBLE TOPICS FOR DISCUSSION
Most will offer things about chores or school work. Ask for things regarding friends, self.

HINTS
1. Some things will have an irrational base; let children list them anyway.
2. Be prepared to hear items about yourself as a teacher.
3. This activity will give children space to move past blaming others if they may do so unconditionally.

TIME
20–30 minutes.

ACTIVITY #5
I HAVE TO. . .

OBJECTIVES
1. To allow children to make others responsible for themselves.

2. To develop ground work for the remainder of the activities concerning responsibility.

MATERIALS NEEDED
Paper and pencil for each child and an adequate place to write.

INSTRUCTIONS
1. Ask children to put the heading "I have to" at the top of their paper.
2. For about ten minutes, allow children to list all the things they "have" to do.
3. Without giving specific answers, suggest general topics such as home, school, or friends.
4. When children seem in a good stopping place, ask them to share what they "have" to do.
5. Collect papers to be used in the next exercise.

POSSIBLE TOPICS FOR DISCUSSION
1. There are a lot of people in the world telling us what to do.
2. We like some things we "have" to do, and dislike others.

HINTS
1. This exercise allows for full expression of putting blame on others. It is the basis for the next exercise, which is claiming all responsibility.
2. Be aware of children blaming classmates in a critical, harmful way.

TIME
25 minutes.

I CHOOSE TO. . .

OBJECTIVES
1. To give children a different perspective on being responsible for themselves.
2. To give children the responsibility to accept or reject the following information.

MATERIALS NEEDED
1. Paper and pencils for each child.
2. Lists used in Exercise #5—Building Responsibility.

INSTRUCTIONS
1. Ask each child to put at the top of his paper "I choose to."
2. Tell them that you are going to help them out by returning their previously made "I have to" lists.
3. Explain that you know they may not believe what they are writing, but to please copy the list word for word on the "I have to" page.
4. When children are finished, share complete sentences from willing class members.
5. Choose one of the most common topics, such as doing school work, and discuss with the children how they make decisions regarding their school work. They could refuse to do it, but would be unwilling to accept the consequences.

POSSIBLE TOPICS FOR DISCUSSION
1. If we like doing something, it does not seem like a "have to" situation.
2. We do not have to like something to "choose" to do it.

HINTS

If you present this as information to be used at the child's discretion, you will get better results than if you attempt to force them to accept it.

TIME

25–30 minutes

OTHER ALTERNATIVES

OBJECTIVES

1. To offer children the opportunity to make selective decisions about their lives.
2. To offer information that will help children think constructively about alternatives.

MATERIALS NEEDED

None

INSTRUCTIONS

1. Have children join together in a circle for a group discussion.
2. Begin a discussion about a true or fictitious event concerning people.
3. Guide the discussion so children can begin to realize that there are alternatives in our behavior, and that we decide what that behavior will be.
4. Encourage children to offer all possible alternatives, even extreme ones.

POSSIBLE TOPICS FOR DISCUSSION

1. Our lives and actions are our own responsibilities.

2. Thinking things out helps in choosing the best alternatives for each of us.

HINTS
1. Be aware of children who try to get you to make the correct or best choices and then agree.
2. Be accepting and positive about all you hear.

TIME
20–30 minutes.

ACTIVITY #8

FANTASY (IF I COULD, I WOULD)

OBJECTIVES
1. To enjoy a guided fantasy.
2. To give children the opportunity to fantasize about their lives.
3. To offer information about how to move closer to our dreams and make them reality.

MATERIALS NEEDED
Space for each child to lie down comfortably.

INSTRUCTIONS
1. Have children find a comfortable place to lie on the floor and relax.
2. Ask them to close their eyes and take long, deep breaths.
3. Give children permission to let their minds wander, stopping to ponder a thought for a moment or two, and then moving on.
4. When the group seems to be ready, begin a narrative in your own words and style based upon the following:

Today is a very special day because as we relax and think, we are going to allow ourselves to dream about those things we wish could be different in the world—in our own world.

(Pause)

Allow yourself to think about things in your life that you would change. Perhaps these things concern home, school, your friends, teachers, or yourselves.

(Pause)

Let your mind move from one of these areas to another, pausing to think of your changes and then moving on.

(Pause)

Perhaps one of your "If I Could, I Would's" keeps returning to your thoughts. If so, stay with it for a while.

(Pause)

As you think of this change, keep in mind that you are responsible for your life and all that happens to you. Take long, deep breaths as you use that responsibility to determine your changes.

(Pause)

Let all the ways to make changes become a part of your thinking now. Allow them to become you and all that you are. These kinds of thoughts are tools to give you the ability to make those "If I Could, I Would's" into real happenings in your life.

(Pause)

When you are in a comfortable place in your thoughts, allow yourself to return to this place. Open your eyes slowly, allowing the room to warm you, not startle you.

5. When everyone appears to be present, ask them to share their experiences with a person close by or with the entire group.

POSSIBLE TOPICS FOR DISCUSSION
1. Any aspect of the fantasy can be discussed.
2. Sometimes dreams do come true.

HINTS
1. Be slow and soothing in your presentation.
2. Use your own style.

TIME
30 minutes.

ACTIVITY #9
FOLLOW-UP ON FANTASY

OBJECTIVES
1. To bring children to a conclusion concerning the fantasy.
2. To represent our dreams visually and orally.

MATERIALS NEEDED
Any art medium suitable for the age group.

INSTRUCTIONS
1. Ask children to represent their dream or some part of the fantasy through the use of the art medium.
2. Allow children to share if they would like.
3. If appropriate, display the children's works.
   (This art project will probably have no need for discussion. Most children will be engrossed in their thoughts.)

TIME
30 minutes.

ACTIVITY #10

"I HOPE I AM—
AM NOT"

OBJECTIVES

1. To create an environment that allows free self-expression of ideals.
2. To allow children to "be" now and not wait until the future.
3. To develop a deeper appreciation of one's self.

MATERIALS NEEDED

Paper and pencils for each child.

INSTRUCTIONS

1. Ask children to write across the top of their paper the words "When I grow up . . . "
2. Have them make two columns which are continuations to this sentence. One is headed "I hope I am," and the other, "I hope I am not."
3. Allow about five to ten minutes for them to make a list of the things they hope they are.
4. Give children an opportunity to share. Reinforce using the complete sentence "When I grow up, I hope I am . . . "
5. When sharing is finished, allow another five to ten minutes to complete the second list.
6. Again allow time for sharing using the complete sentence.
7. After this sharing, ask children to mark out the words "When I grow up." Give time for sharing these new sentences.
8. Now ask them to take out the words "I Hope" in each column, and to read this new set of sentences to themselves. Allow time for sharing.

9. Stress to children that they are these things now, that magic does not happen at a certain age to change them. Encourage them to accept themselves as what their list says and to experience those things right now.
10. Close with volunteers reading one thing from their lists.

POSSIBLE TOPICS FOR DISCUSSION
Those that projected occupations or aspects of adulthood are preparing to be and do those things right now.

HINTS
1. This is a powerful exercise for fifth and sixth graders.
2. Tell children they can alter or add to their list at any time.

TIME
45–50 minutes.

ACTIVITY #11

REASONS FOR BEHAVIOR

OBJECTIVES
1. To inform students of how people react according to their personal circumstances.
2. To give children permission to make decisions for themselves, and not for the sake of others.

MATERIALS NEEDED
Paper and pencil for each child.

INSTRUCTIONS
1. Tell children you are going to read them a list of behaviors that may happen daily.

2. Ask them to write down the reason for that behavior. A few words will do, so they can remember for the discussion to follow.
3. Include situations that are relevant to your school and your classroom. Examples of such things are:
   (a) Child comes to school angry.
   (b) Best friend forgets your birthday.
   (c) Parent jumps on a child for no apparent reason.
   (d) Student seems happy about everything.
   (e) Teacher is unfair to class.
   (f) Someone who is outgoing is not talking today.
   (g) You cannot seem to concentrate on what is happening around you.
   (h) One of your classmates sits in the back of the room crying softly.
4. Include other situations if necessary.
5. Ask children to share each reason they saw for the behavior.
6. Ask children to give their own reasons for having the behavior.

POSSIBLE TOPICS FOR DISCUSSION
1. All behavior has a reason.
2. People react differently.
3. We are responsible for the behavior we choose in each situation.

HINTS
1. Give children permission to maintain their chosen behavior for as long as they need to continue it, just so they are not infringing on someone else's rights.
2. If any child refuses to be responsible for his actions, be open and accepting of him. Ask him if he is willing to be responsible for not being responsible.

TIME
30 minutes.

ACTIVITY #12

ONE TIME YES—ONE TIME NO

OBJECTIVES
1. To discuss how we may react differently to the same situation.
2. To offer information about decisions in regard to our behavior.
3. To teach children to be responsible for their own behaviors.

MATERIALS NEEDED
None

INSTRUCTIONS
1. Divide the class into four or five small groups.
2. Begin by talking about how things sometimes make us mad and other times do not bother us at all.
3. Ask children to relate to each other similar experiences they have had.
4. Join the groups back together. Again share among one another how this phenomenon occurs.
5. Tell children that we decide how a set of circumstances is going to affect us and then react accordingly.
6. Give children permission to think of other ways they might have reacted to the same stimuli.

POSSIBLE TOPICS FOR DISCUSSION
1. It is most valuable to react to situations in the simplest, smoothest way possible for our lives.

115

2. We are responsible for our actions and reactions, and can make positive decisions about the outcome of these situations.

HINTS

Children may resist this responsibility. Give them permission to accept what they are able to process for themselves.

TIME

30 minutes.

ACTIVITY #13

WHO IS RESPONSIBLE? (BLAMING)*

OBJECTIVES

1. To give children the opportunity to deny all responsibility for their actions.
2. To give children the opportunity to accept all responsibility for their actions.
3. To experience teacher's self-disclosing.

MATERIALS NEEDED

None

INSTRUCTIONS

1. Join the class in a circle for a discussion.

*This activity appeared in a slightly different form in *Transpersonal Communication*, by Barry K. Weinhold and Lynn C. Elliott (Englewood Cliffs, N.J.: Prentice-Hall, Inc., 1979), p. 66. Permission to reprint is gratefully acknowledged.

2. Have a particular, personal incident ready to share with the children.
3. Tell them that you will share a story with them twice.
4. The first time you share this story, blame everything that happened to you on anyone and everything else around you.
5. Repeat the story, owning responsibility for everything that happened.
6. Ask the children to discuss how these two stories are different.
7. Children need to find a partner and do the same kind of experience relating with each other.
8. When each partner has had an opportunity to share, join back together for insights that the children may have developed through this exercise.

POSSIBLE TOPICS FOR DISCUSSION
1. It is much easier to blame others than to be totally responsible.
2. We can do something about our own actions, but nothing about others' actions.

HINTS
Children may not see how they can be responsible for things that happen around them (weather, car out of control, someone else pushing them). Encourage them to think about why they chose to be in a situation.

TIME
30 minutes.

ACTIVITY #14*

HOW CAN I MAKE YOU?

OBJECTIVES
1. To reinforce the concept of self-responsibility.
2. To discuss the irrational belief that someone "makes" another person do something.

MATERIALS NEEDED
None

INSTRUCTIONS
1. Join the group together for a discussion.
2. Think of statements with the children that include the concept of being made to do something, such as:
   (a) He makes me laugh when he acts silly.
   (b) It makes me mad when people interrupt me.
   (c) My friend made me get into a fight.
3. Children will have plenty of these kinds of statements. Allow them to discuss them for a while and then ask simply, "How?"
4. Lead the discussion toward the realization that the only time we are "made" is when we are physically forced (tickling or hitting).
5. Help them to realize that they are choosing to be angry or to laugh. They are responsible for their own lives and actions.

*Weinhold/Elliott, *Transpersonal Communication*, © 1979, p. 66. Adapted from Elliott, "Centering in Feeling and Communication," in Hendricks and Roberts, *The Second Centering Book*, © 1977, pp. 109–111. Reprinted by permission of Prentice-Hall, Inc., Englewood Cliffs, New Jersey.

6. As a closing exercise ask them to repeat their original statements changing them to "I am responsible for . . . "

POSSIBLE TOPICS FOR DISCUSSION

Children have the ability to decide what part they will play in an experience, and thus be responsible for that experience.

HINTS

After this exercise, reinforce this concept in all activities and interactions on a daily basis.

TIME

30–45 minutes.

ACTIVITY #15

STRAIGHT STATEMENTS

OBJECTIVES

1. To give children information about communicating wants and needs in a straightforward way.
2. To teach children how indirect statements are misunderstood.
3. To teach children that adults or friends are not mind readers.

MATERIALS NEEDED

None

INSTRUCTIONS

1. Bring children together for a group discussion.
2. Tell children how we need to state our wants and needs in an honest, open manner. Discuss.

3. Tell them that teachers, friends, and parents have no magical powers to guess what the need or want is.
4. Encourage them to discuss how they are responsible to communicate what they are feeling in an effective way.
5. Give examples of how unclear messages keep us from getting what we want or need. Begin with simple examples and move to whatever complex ones the groups can handle. The following are examples of actions or statements, to be followed by a brief discussion:
   (a) Child holds up foot with untied shoe.
   (b) "I can't find my pencil."
   (c) "My paper is a mess."
   (d) "Everyone picks on me."
   (e) "Tell her to leave me alone."
   (f) "I don't know how to do this."
6. Discuss how each of these things have hidden meanings.
7. Encourage children to examine how time and energy is wasted trying to discover these meanings.
8. With the children, think of more appropriate and easier ways to get these wants and needs.

POSSIBLE TOPICS FOR DISCUSSION

We do not always show what we want or need. That is okay, but we cannot expect others to figure these things out for us.

HINTS

1. Use this reinforcement as you interact with children and they interact with each other.
2. Help them to talk to each other without your mediating.

TIME

20 minutes.

7

building self-esteem

In this section of the Curriculum For Consciousness we focus on ways students can build self-esteem. There are fewer activities in this section because the reader can find many more in another Prentice-Hall book entitled, *100 Ways to Enhance Self-Concept in the Classroom,* by Jack Canfield and Harold Wells. This excellent volume is complementary to all the materials in this book, and comes highly recommended to all creative teachers.

ACTIVITY #1
THINGS YOU DO WELL

OBJECTIVES
To offer children an opportunity to think positively about themselves.

MATERIALS NEEDED
Paper and pencil for each child.

INSTRUCTIONS
1. Give paper to each person.
2. Ask them to make a list of ten things they do well.
3. Share the list with the group.

POSSIBLE TOPICS FOR DISCUSSION
1. It feels good to like oneself.
2. Was it difficult to think of ten things?

HINTS
1. When children share, encourage listening by others who may disagree.
2. Encourage children who have a difficult time to take it one step at a time.
3. Give the children permission to like themselves.

TIME
20 minutes.

ACTIVITY #2
FEELING GOOD

OBJECTIVES
1. To allow children to examine their world and find the good parts in it.
2. To develop discrimination and priorities.

MATERIALS NEEDED
Paper and pencils.

INSTRUCTIONS
1. Give children paper.
2. Ask them to make a list of ten things that make them feel good each day.
3. When all are finished, allow time for sharing.

POSSIBLE TOPICS FOR DISCUSSION
1. Were any things the same as on the first list?
2. Where does "feeling good" happen inside of us?
3. Our environment (home, parents, other people) influence how we feel.

HINTS
1. Make a list and share it.
2. Give children positive strokes and permission to think for themselves.

TIME
25 minutes.

ACTIVITY #3
YOUR TEN BEST THINGS

OBJECTIVES
1. To let children express through art things they like best.
2. To give children the opportunity for self-awareness.

MATERIALS NEEDED
1. Drawing paper for each child.
2. Paint, crayons, or other means of providing color.

INSTRUCTIONS
1. See that each child has the needed art supplies.

2. Ask the children to draw a picture of the ten things they like to do best, using words, pictures, or both.

3. When most children have finished, allow volunteers to share their ten most fun things to do.

POSSIBLE TOPICS FOR DISCUSSION

1. It is good to do the things we like as often as possible.
2. Do all people have to like doing the same things to get along?

HINTS

1. Be sure the children do ten different things and not a continuation of one.
2. Do not be critical of art work. Children will worry if their work is right or wrong.

TIME

30 minutes.

ACTIVITY #4

OTHER PEOPLE LIKE ME BECAUSE . . .

OBJECTIVES

1. To allow children to integrate support from others.
2. To encourage children to recognize how others feel about them, and what value this information has for them.
3. To heighten self-esteem.

MATERIALS NEEDED

Paper and pencil.

INSTRUCTIONS

1. Ask children to write down a list of things about themselves that other people like.

2. Allow sharing of the lists by volunteers. Be sure they are using the complete sentence, "People like me because. . ."

POSSIBLE TOPICS FOR DISCUSSION
1. Sometimes we do not like what others seem to like.
2. Realization of our importance seems to be hidden until we have it pointed out to us.

HINTS
Do this exercise with the children.

TIME
30 minutes.

ACTIVITY #5

HOW OTHERS HELP ME FEEL GOOD

OBJECTIVES
1. To make distinctions about the actions of others that we like.
2. To help children realize that they can find people that help them feel good.

MATERIALS NEEDED
Paper and pencil.

INSTRUCTIONS
1. Ask the children to relax and think of all the things that other people do that make them feel good.
2. Encourage them to think of all the people with whom they have contact, and what those people do to create good feelings.
3. When everyone has thought for a while, ask them to list all those good things.

4. All willing children can share a few of these good things.
5. State in closing that we make decisions to be around people that cause us good or bad feelings.

POSSIBLE TOPICS FOR DISCUSSION

Why would we choose to be around people who stir up unpleasant feelings?

HINTS

No one has control over our feelings except us. It is our responsibility to seek out those people who help us experience ourselves at a comfortable level.

TIME

20 minutes.

8

centering and relaxation

In this section of the Curriculum for Consciousness we focus on centering and relaxation. Because centering activities are covered thoroughly in earlier books, we will offer only several examples of these types of activities here. For dozens of other centering activities, see *The Centering Book, The Second Centering Book,* and *The Family Centering Book,* all published by Prentice-Hall, Inc.*

A BASIC CENTERING ACTIVITY

This exercise can be used any time there is a need for students to become relaxed yet alert. It takes about 10 to 15 minutes, and is best done lying down with eyes closed.

*If you would like a 6-cassette program of relaxation and centering activities I have made for use in classrooms, you can order it for $30 from me at the University of Colorado, Colorado Springs, Colorado 80907.

INSTRUCTIONS

Find yourself a good position to be in for a few minutes, a position where your body feels comfortable and relaxed. Relax and close your eyes.

(Pause 5–10 seconds)

Let your body begin to relax and slow down. You might imagine it becoming loose, warm, relaxed, and heavy. Picture it sinking down into itself, relaxing into itself, letting it be completely supported by the floor.

(Pause 10–20 seconds)

As you relax, notice your breathing as it flows in and out of your body. Just feel the breath coming in and out of your body.

(Pause 10–20 seconds)

Now rest your right hand on your stomach over your navel, and rest your left hand on your chest, just under your collarbone. Relax for a while and rest.

(Pause 1–5 minutes)

Now you can relax your arms at your sides again, noticing the feelings and sensations in your body. Let your mind play in the quiet space as your body feels rested and alert.

(Pause 10–15 seconds)

Now we will return our awareness to the room. We will count down from 10 to 1, and as I get closer to 1 you can feel more and more alert. When I get to 1, open your eyes and sit up, feeling rested and alert. 10-9-8-7-6-5-4-3-2-1. Sit up, feeling rested and alert.

A BASIC RELAXATION ACTIVITY

This exercise takes 10 to 15 minutes, and can be used before tests or anytime a calming influence is needed. It can be done either seated or lying down.

INSTRUCTIONS

Close your eyes and put your body in a relaxed position for a few minutes. Move around until you are comfortable.
(Pause 10–15 seconds)
Lift your right arm up until you feel some tension in it. Just hold it for a moment and notice the tension.
(Pause 10 seconds)
Now let it relax. Feel all the tension drain out of it. Let it feel completely supported.
(Pause 10–15 seconds)
Lift your left arm until you feel tension.
(Pause 10 seconds)
Now let it go, letting it relax completely.
(Pause 10–15 seconds)
Lift your right leg until you feel some tension in it.
(Pause 10 seconds)
Good. Now relax it completely.
(Pause 10–15 seconds)
Raise your left leg until you feel tension in it.
(Pause 10 seconds)
Now let it relax completely, supported by the floor.
(Pause 10–15 seconds)
Imagine your whole body lifting up until you feel tension in it.
(Pause 10 seconds)
Now let it relax and sink back down into itself.
(Repeat the last two instructions 1 to 3 times)
Rest for a moment and enjoy the feeling of relaxed alertness.
(Pause 1–3 minutes)
Now we will be coming back to awareness of the room. As I count from ten to one, you will feel more and more alert, and when I get to 1, you will open your eyes, feeling relaxed and alert. 10-9-8-7-6-5-4-3-2-1, open your eyes, feeling rested and alert.

A MENTAL RELAXATION
ACTIVITY

This activity makes use of the mind's power to bring about feelings of calm alertness. It takes 5–10 minutes and can be done seated or lying down.

INSTRUCTIONS

Let your body and mind relax for a moment. Close your eyes and rest in the quiet of yourself.
(Pause 10–15 seconds)
Think of a soft, golden light down in the center of your body. It is a gentle light that grows with each breath you take. With each breath your light gets stronger and brighter.
(Pause 3 or 4 breaths)
Now imagine the golden light filling your chest and heart.
(Pause 5 seconds)
Imagine the golden light filling your mind. Feel it shining out from your whole body. The light shines from your arms, legs, chest, stomach—all of you.
(Pause 10 seconds)
Now let us fill up the whole room with our light.
(Pause 10 seconds)
Now the whole world.
(Pause 10 seconds)
Let your light come back to rest in you.
(Pause 10–15 seconds)
Now, when you feel ready, you can open your eyes again, feeling rested and alert.

three

centering
in special education,
reading,
and administration

introduction

In this section we see how the concepts and activities of centering can be applied to special education, reading, and administration. The use of centering has been well described in such areas as counseling (see Ivey and Simek, 1980), social studies, mathematics, and language (see Hendricks and Fadiman, 1976), but until now there has been little discussion of the use of centering in the three areas to be examined here. I asked colleagues George Karius, Pam Mills, and Peg Bacon, each specialists in the three areas, to prepare chapters on their fields of expertise. I believe that each of these articles is brilliant and makes an important and lasting contribution to education.

centering in special education

Pamela Jean Mills, Ph.D.

Since the implementation of Public Law 94-142, the Education of Handicapped Children's Act of 1975, classroom teachers have been faced with a greater number of children with special learning and behavioral needs. These needs have demanded much of the teachers' time, skills, and energy. Adjustments in curriculum, materials, methods, and the physical environment have been necessary within the regular class to accommodate and instruct the child with special needs.

Teachers who were once told to refer for special education evaluation any children who caused behavioral or academic difficulty are now informed that these same children are their own responsibilities. Teachers are expected to increase their skills to accommodate children with a wider variety of learning needs and problems.

The types of problems teachers must handle include the entire gamut of learning handicaps from mild to in some cases, severe. Problems including learning disabilities, mental retardation, emotional disturbance, visual and auditory impairments, and even some physical disabilities can be expected in a classroom. Hopefully not all of these problems will present themselves in any one classroom at the same time, but the possibility of a teacher encountering one or more of them yearly is increasing. The better we can identify problems early and begin proper remediation and instruction, the more likely children with severe and specific learning difficulties will be found in a regular classroom during the elementary grades.

In order to deal more effectively with the ever increasing number and variety of children with special learning needs, teachers must look beyond regular strategies for techniques successful in aiding children to deal with their own problems. Centering is such a technique. Activities to enable children to relax, reduce anxiety, control their own anger, hostility, and impulses, to concentrate longer, and foster visual stimulation will assist the classroom teacher in mainstreaming children with learning problems. Teaching the child self-help skills can leave the teacher free to help others. The emotionally disturbed child who can learn to anticipate and prevent outbursts of anger, the learning disabled child who can learn to inhibit and control his own impulses, and the mentally retarded child who can learn to increase his concentration skills and use visual imagery to assist in retaining information can lessen the time the teacher needs to devote to these specific problems and leave the teacher available to work on other difficulties. The child with emotional problems who has learned to use fantasy as a tool rather than an escape mechanism is on the road to coping with his own problems.

Centering activities offer the possibility for accommodating a wide variety of learning needs and problems within the same classroom. A "centered teacher" with "centered students" can extend the range of normality to accept the learner who has difficulties. Whether the problem is academic or behavioral, centering activities can be used to foster personal growth and development and, by the very nature of centering, enhance individualization of instruction. Activities should be designed and utilized according to the nature of the needs and the severity of the problems. Through trial and error or direct systematic intervention, the classroom teacher can use the philosophy and activities of centering to assist children and youth in coping more effectively with special learning problems and to remediate those problems whenever possible. Centering is an exciting methodology for assisting the handicapped learner within the regular classroom.

TEACHING STRATEGIES

For children with special needs, teachers must adopt centering exercises to assure the participation of all students. Many of the same adaptations necessary for centering activities will also be beneficial for basic classroom instruction. A few of these adaptations are discussed here.

Language

For all instruction it is important to use language within the child's receptive and expressive vocabulary. The child needs to be able to fully understand what is expected (receptive language) and then to be able to follow whatever directions have been given (expressive language). Although we often assume a child's physical size is indicative of his or her facility with language (words), this is often untrue for children with special learning needs. So often language impairment accompanies or causes the learning difficulty and the child is unable to comprehend or express himself at age level. Careful analysis of language level is a prerequisite to using centering activities with the handicapped learner.

Sequencing Instruction and Directions

In order to maximize the learning potential for each student, directions need to be sequenced such that they can be followed by all students. In many cases, teachers will need to begin by giving one direction at a time and checking to see that all children are following it before giving further instructions. (Teachers should be aware of students who are "nodders" and not assume that just because a student smiles and nods he knows what is expected of him.)

The use of sequencing is important so that students can begin with simple instruction and advance only when they are ready. By building upon earlier skill development, students can be assured of understanding what is necessary for the activities. Going from simple to complex, both in the directions and in the activities themselves, can foster optimal participation and growth on the part of the students.

Buddy System

A technique that allows for participation of handicapped learners within the educational mainstream is that of the buddy system. By allowing children to work with other children, teachers can be free to work with other students and be assured that the instruction and activities will be completed.

The student with auditory problems needs a "listening buddy" to help him understand what has been said and what is to be done. The child with visual impairment can often be aided by a "sighted buddy," one who can be his "eyes" and assist in orientation and mobility during the activities. Children who are slow learners can also be aided by working with children who are "good" at the activities, and this can be helpful for those who are high achievers and enjoy teaching.

It is a well-known but little understood phenomenon that children can often teach other children that teachers have difficulty in reaching. Whether or not it is due to the fact that the children "speak the same language" or that they have just recently learned the activity themselves, children are often the best teachers.

Demonstration

Due to the often reduced language ability of the handicapped learners or to the difficulty in following directions, demonstration often becomes a key factor in teaching children who experience difficulty in learning. If children can see either the teacher or other children actually performing the activity, they can be more assured of what is actually being asked and are often more willing to participate. Handicapped learners often hesitate in participation because they are often frustrated by their inability to perform as well as the other children, and because of the failure that often accompanies their performance. Demonstration to get the children started on an activity can be a useful technique to insure maximum participation of everyone.

No Right or Wrong Way

Students need to know that there is no absolute way of doing the centering activities. They need to know that full participation is the desired goal, rather than some specific response. The very nature of centering activities allows for freedom of response, and students should not be condemned for trying. There is no one right way, or no really wrong way, to perform most of the activities. The child's performance is based on personal ability level and takes into account the particular learning handicap of the student. Varying the activity to accommodate learning problems can help assure that all students benefit from the activity.

Appropriate Setting
In addition to adaptations required in the instructions, sequencing, and evaluation, students with handicaps may require a different or modified space in order to be able to participate fully in centering activities. Some of the activities may require a quiet space where the child who is easily distracted can be alone. A quiet corner that is available by student choice can provide the space necessary for children who cannot tolerate distractions. This space should be designed by the students themselves and open to all students. Going to the quiet corner should not be viewed as a penalty, but as an opportunity.

An activity space should also be made available. This needs to be an area in which students can move freely, and in which furniture, lighting, and other children do not inhibit the students' movements. Ample space should be provided, with carpeting if there is the possibility of students falling and hurting themselves.

By considering the nature of the handicaps of the children involved, teachers can use logic and common teaching sense to help them adapt the centering activities to meet the children's needs. By "experiencing" the handicap themselves, teachers can more readily adapt the environment and instruction to meet the needs of all children within their classes. Teachers also need to remember that the activities are not absolute in themselves and that any necessary adjustments can be made.

In the following section, types of activities for use with the handicapped within the regular classroom will be discussed. For each type of activity, the purpose, target audience, and examples of activities will be included. Classroom teachers can use these as a guide for developing their own activities based on the children they are teaching. Each child's needs are somewhat unique and, therefore, the activities must be individualized by using the principles involved in centering and the goal for instruction of the child. Teachers can develop their own list of activities to supplement the ones discussed in Part II of this book, as well as *The Centering Book* and *The Second Centering Book.*

CENTERING ACTIVITIES

It is important that all lessons in centering begin with a relaxation period in which the students and teacher(s) can quiet their bodies and clear their minds. This is an important step for all concerned. The classroom often causes anxiety in children, particularly in those who have difficulty with regular instruction. Turning down the lights and/or closing the shades can help to set the mood for a relaxed atmosphere and help to eliminate any tension that might be present.

Relaxation

Purpose. Children who experience difficulty in learning are often tense when working within the classroom. These children should be taught to recognize the times when they would probably tense up and to actively work at either preventing or reducing these feelings. Children can be taught to focus on themselves and concentrate on their center when they feel themselves tightening up. Simple awareness of physical signs of anxiety and tenseness can help the child to relax at a time in which he would normally respond another way.

Relaxation activities can be done at predetermined times of the day or whenever the child knows he needs to relax. They can be done individually, with a partner, or as part of a small or large group. Space needs to be made available so the child is not conspicuous while doing the activities, as additional attention is probably something he needs least.

Target Audience. Relaxation can be very useful for all children, but particularly for the child who is hyperactive, emotionally disturbed, has sensory impairments (visual or auditory), or who stutters. Hyperactive and emotionally disturbed children need to learn relaxation techniques to calm themselves and/or to inhibit behavior. They need to consciously focus on themselves and their behavior, and learn to channel impulsive and aggressive behavior.

Children who have auditory or visual impairments often have to rely on basically one sensory mode for input of information. Due to the extreme concentration required in order to learn through either the eyes or ears alone, children with these handicaps need to learn to relax periodically. Learning can be tiring for any child, but particularly for the child who is limited in ways of gaining information. The child who has to rely mainly on his ears for receiving information is not bombarded with stimulation and must pay particular attention to the information he is hearing. Listening is a tiring experience and frequent breaks coupled with relaxation exercises will help allow the child to concentrate more.

The child who has impaired hearing must rely mainly on his eyes for receiving information and if the classroom environment and instruction are not set up to facilitate his seeing, constant strain and anxiety can prevail. Most of us can tune in and out of the instruction taking place and still are able to gain most of the information. The child without hearing cannot stop looking for fear that he will miss vital information. He must always be alert for things so that he has a chance of knowing what is going on and what is expected of him. Such demand for concentration is tiring and often anxiety-causing in itself.

Activities.   The relaxation activities discussed in *The Centering Book* and *The Second Centering Book,* as well as those in Part II of the present volume, are good for use with all children, including the handicapped. Both the deep relaxation and the instant relaxation activities would be useful for the handicapped child who needs to completely relax his body prior to beginning or continuing class activities. The "meditating, relaxing, and energizing" activities listed in *The Second Centering Book* can be used to recoup some of the energy drained through concentration and to inhibit the impulsiveness of some students. Teachers can vary these activities to meet their own classes' needs, although many should be directly applicable to all.

Movement

Purpose.   Handicapped children often have one of two kinds of difficulty with movement. They either move too much or in inappropriate ways, or are inhibited in their movement and avoid any type of activity that might draw attention to themselves. Movement centering activities can help in both of these instances. For the child who moves too much or in inappropriate ways, the teacher can structure movement activities to teach "proper" movement. By having the child focus on what his body is doing, the teacher can help him to feel the instances in which extraneous movement is not appropriate or to even realize that he is moving. (Some hyperactive children move without even knowing they are doing so, like the child who has been told to stay seated but is halfway to the pencil sharpener before he realizes he has left his seat.)

An awareness of the body is a prerequisite to knowing whether or not you are moving. The child who rocks back and forth, the child who constantly taps his pencil against the side of his desk, or the child who is constantly out of his seat without any specific purpose in mind is not really aware of his actions. These responses have become automatic and without thought. The child needs to learn to focus on this movement and to control it. There are appropriate ways in which the child can move and he needs to be given this opportunity. Movement should not be restricted, but should be brought under self-control and done with a purpose in mind.

In contrast to the child who moves at random or without thought is the child who is inhibited in movement. Some children avoid any movement, either for the purpose of not drawing attention to themselves or because they are not relaxed enough to enjoy the movement. Children who bottle up tension within themselves need to learn to use movement as an inner release and need to be provided activities in which movement is an appropriate release. (In these cases it is often useful to combine relaxation activities with movement activities, so as to both relieve tenseness and to encourage activity.)

Children who avoid movement so as not to draw attention to themselves often feel self-conscious about either their bodies or their ability to perform like their peers. For these children, movement activities need to focus on the activity itself, rather than on specific performance, and standards for correctness of movement need to be eliminated. Children need the opportunity to explore what their bodies can do without getting hung up on whether or not they are as good as their peers.

Target Audience. Children who experience difficulty in movement may suffer from learning disabilities, emotional disturbance, mental retardation, or sensory impairments. Children who are hyperactive or who employ random movement can benefit from activity periods in which they can "burn off excess steam." They need to be allowed or even encouraged to engage in movement activities that will allow them to use excess energy within appropriate situations. By structuring periods of physical activity, teachers can help to ensure that students will engage in activities that will assist in energy release and the children will then be better able to concentrate on desired assignments.

Extraneous movements are common among children who are blind. Blind children do not know how these movements appear to others and need to be taught to inhibit movement that will draw negative attention to themselves. (It is often the differences in behavior that make other students leary of interacting with the blind, rather than the blindness itself. An awareness of inappropriate behavior is a starting point for making the blind student less conspicuous and more acceptable within a regular classroom.)

Mentally retarded children who have been either institutionalized or who have been in self-contained special education classrooms have also often developed inappropriate movement patterns. As in the case of blind students, the mentally retarded need to be aware of what they are doing and be taught acceptable substitute patterns. By being given the impetus to inhibit movement while at the same time being taught appropriate behaviors, the mentally retarded student can become more accepted by other students. Remember that it is not the retardation that has caused this movement to be present, but the lack of appropriate models for behavior and/or the lack of opportunity for directed movement. Some children have learned to self-stimulate or to release energy through random movement, and once the reasons for the inappropriate movement have been removed, students are less readily identified as being different.

Activities. The activities used with movement as a purpose can be divided into three types: the first to inhibit inappropriate movement, the second to release excess energy, and the third to develop skills within movement. All can and should be used to assist the handicapped learner within the regular class.

Inhibited movement involves those activities that will enable children who move without thinking to become aware of and control their movements. The classroom teacher needs to develop ways for the child to monitor his own movement, although this may be a step far along the continuum of self-control. Perhaps by either the teacher monitoring the inappropriate movement or a buddy working with the student, others can be used to help determine the extent of extraneous movement and any patterns related to it. There may be only certain times of the day when the movement is really apparent or when the child uses the movement without awareness. If so, the timing for intervention would be as important as the activities themselves.

When the release of excess energy is the focus, activities need to be employed that will allow the students to engage in appropriate movement without fear of teacher dissatisfaction. One kind of movement that has been related to better student performance is jogging. Many teachers have found that if their students jog daily it can help release excess energy, have a calming influence, and help with academic performance. Numerous studies have shown that jogging for as little as ten minutes a day can have a tremendous effect on classroom performance. (It has also been shown that it is beneficial if the teachers jog along with their students.)

This form of activity has been used for years, with teachers telling students who could not settle down for work to "go run it off." By allowing for systematic jogging for students, teachers can help to eliminate the need for release of excess energy and students will soon learn that there are ways in which they can control their own need for release.

In addition to learning ways to release excess energy, some students will need to develop skills for moving. One way of doing this is to employ what has been referred to as basic movement lessons in which the student is taught to explore the ways in which his body can move and then to move in ways which are best for him. Another advantage to basic movement exercises is that little equipment and/ or alteration of classroom environment is necessary. By simply moving back the desks in the classroom, the teacher can provide adequate space for exploring body movement.

The purpose of basic movement exercises is to develop the body's ability to move and to develop full awareness of movement possibilities. There is no right or wrong way for the child to move and even the physically handicapped or the particularly clumsy child can learn to move to the best of his ability. By exploring alternatives for achieving basic movement skills, the child can develop skills to his own level and is not forced to compete with more competent or less disabled children.

By using the centering books and any good text on basic movement activities (Cratty, 1980; Logsdon & Barrett, 1969) the classroom teacher can employ movement as an activity for centering with children who need it. There are almost limitless possibilities for using movement within the classroom and the teachers need only to look to their classes and outside resources to identify the possibilities for use. Movement activities are essential to help children learn to inhibit extraneous movement or to develop movement skills, and they should become a part of any daily routine for the children.

Visual Imagery

Purpose. Children with learning difficulties often have problems when asked to visualize material or to use visual imagery as a technique to aid remembering. Creative thinking seems to be lacking in many children and often it is the lack of visual imagery that inhibits their creative exploration. These activities can be used as a way to enhance the thinking ability of children who need to deal on a concrete learning level or who need to think beyond what they have available for direct learning. Visual imagery can be used as an instructional aid to facilitate divergent and creative thinking.

Target Audience. The mentally retarded child is often identified as one who has to rely on concrete information and who is inhibited in dealing with abstract ideas or thoughts. These children are often identified as having little imagination and being tied to what can be seen. Regardless of whether or not these accusations are correct, visual imagery activities in which the child is guided in using his imagination can be useful. (Not many of us could quickly identify the number of windows in our homes, but many could correctly count the windows if given a "guided tour" of the premises.)

The blind are also inhibited in using visual imagery, often because teachers hesitate to have the children "see" pictures. When working with children who once had sight but have since lost it, teachers need to build upon the memories the children have of what they once saw and use language to stimulate thought and images. When working with children who have never had sight, teachers need to use language and concrete experiences to guide the thought. They should not be afraid to ask the children to visualize their thoughts, but should be ready to assist in whatever ways are possible.

Children with learning disabilities can also benefit from visual imagery activities. These activities can be good for children whose stronger channel is that of vision and who can use them to enhance memory, and for those for whom vision is not a strong channel, but who can improve within this area. We should not avoid using deficit channels for learning, but must use areas of strength to enhance learning within these channels.

Activities. Almost any activity in which the child is taught to get a visual picture and then to use this visual picture for learning can be useful. Teachers can begin by having the child visualize pictures of things they already know and can help the children to identify the detail in the picture. (Teachers should remember to move from the simple to the complex and to lead the children into describing as much detail as possible.) Once the children have mastered the idea of getting visual pictures and describing what they can "see," teachers can then have the children visualize based upon what they are told, and then on what happens at the end of an episode of visual exploration. There should be no exact expectation for what the child will "see" and all images should be accepted according to the ability of the child.

Once the child has the idea of visual imagery, the aspect of centering can be introduced. Children can be taught to feel what they see and to let their images have a direct bearing on their feeling. The activities described in *The Centering Book* are excellent ones for helping children explore the relationship between what they see and how they feel. By allowing children to choose the output for visual imagery centering activities, teachers can help children to identify the ways in which they can best express themselves. Individualization of the activity can be enhanced according to the type of assignment given and the type of reaction expected. All children should not be expected to produce the same type of product.

Fantasy

Purpose. Children have often been identified as having too much fantasy or on relying too much on things that are not real. Yet these same fantasies can facilitate learning and develop skills in other areas. The child who is emotionally disturbed or mentally retarded is often blamed for relying too much on fantasy, which can actually be used to help develop self-control and to take to another level the visual imagery exercises discussed above.

When directed in using fantasy, children can learn to identify for themselves when they are being creative and when they are dealing with what is "real." Children should be taught to fantasize and then to consciously stop the fantasizing. It is this conscious control of behavior that will help the child who has relied on fantasy to recognize and control the difference.

Fantasy activities are great for developing creative thought and for using abstract, rather than concrete, thought. They can be used with children who are just learning to deal with abstractions or who have relied too heavily on a concrete level.

Target Audience. Teachers should help the mentally retarded or very young student to recognize fantasy for what it is (not reality) and to benefit from it. Children can be taught to recognize why their fantasies could not possibly be real and, therefore, begin to learn the realities of existence. Conscious thought about the real and the unreal can help the student realize why some fantasies could not or should not occur. Sometimes students only fantasize partway and they need to be taught to recognize what would really happen should their fantasies become reality.

The emotionally disturbed child also needs to learn to differentiate reality from the dream world and to recognize the differences. Sometimes the use of fantasy can provide a temporary escape mechanism that can help the child get through a bad time or situation, but the child needs to know *when* he is using this fantasy and to control its usage to the proper times. As a temporary escape device it can be useful, but as a consistent method of approach it can further inhibit normal development.

The blind can benefit from the use of fantasy in much the same way in which visual imagery can be useful. Fantasy for the blind student can be a way to expand what is actually taking place, and can be a means of experiencing activities that might prove too difficult given the lack of sight or lack of prerequisite skills. Fantasy can be a good way for the students to experience activities that might be dangerous and, in fact, the fantasy can be used to identify the dangers in different situations.

All children can benefit from the use of fantasy and many experts believe that the use of fantasy is a way for children to accept reality. Conscious thought about the fantasies enables the students to control them. Only when we have complete control over the use of fantasy does it become a learning tool, rather than a means of escape.

Activities. The ways in which fantasy can be used within the classroom are limitless. It can be used with almost any subject matter or in a variety of ways. Movement activities involve fantasy when we ask children to move like a snake or to fly like a bird. We can use the fantasy to ask children to feel different things and then to respond to these feelings. The "Teaching with Fantasy" section of *The Second Centering Book* provides a host of ideas for using fantasy within the class. Using this as a basis, the teacher can then adapt the activities to meet the abilities of the students and the purpose for which the teacher is using the activity.

Prior to using fantasy activities with the class, the teacher will want to be certain that the children are relaxed and are aware of the purpose of the activity. Children will want to know what is expected of them and what is acceptable behavior. The teacher must decide in advance what limitations will be imposed, if any, and why they might be necessary. If students with extreme imaginations or those who already deal too much in a fantasy world are involved, the teacher may want to structure the activity with these students in mind or separate them from participation. Children with extremely aggressive behavior need to use caution in and limit their fantasies so as to not bring out further inappropriate aggression. (Teachers who know that they have children with these tendencies can structure the fantasies to have a calming influence on the students.)

Concentration

Purpose. All children need to learn to concentrate, whether it is to eliminate extraneous stimuli or to gain greater skill for the focusing of attention. Rooms cannot always be quiet or void of other activity and students should learn to perform when conditions are not always best. The tuning out of extraneous information and the tuning in on what is important will allow the child to study wherever he is and to pinpoint only the important data that are presented.

Target Audience. Children with learning disabilities, mental retardation, and sensory impairments are considered to have reduced concentration skills. For the learning disabled and mentally retarded, concentration skills become a way to attend to stimuli that is important to the task at hand. Concentration levels can be increased and extended and even children with extremely limited levels can learn to concentrate more and on the "right" thing.

For the child with impaired auditory or visual acuity to profit from classroom instruction, the focus of the concentration activities becomes a necessity. The child with an impaired sensory acuity must be able to identify and move into the situation that will enhance learning. Open seating for children will allow them to move where they can best learn and to allow for greater concentration. The child who cannot hear or who cannot see must rely primarily on the other mode of input and needs to learn a level of concentration that can be extended for great lengths of time. For this child the inability to tune in and out causes him to need greater levels of concentration. The child needs to consciously relax and focus only on important information.

Activities. Almost any activity that will help the child to focus on particular information and to screen out extraneous stimuli will be useful. Teachers must structure activities that require the children to constantly develop additional concentration skills. By beginning with short assignments with simple detail and then augmenting the time and complexity of detail required, the teacher can build new skills upon existing ones. Great patience and much imagination is required of the teacher, but the end goal of greater concentration is worth the effort. Children with learning handicaps must learn to concentrate within the regular class if they are to learn along with the others.

Summary

There is great similarity between many of the activities and the need for certain activities within specific types of handicaps. The creative and thoughtful teacher will combine and introduce them to the class as a unified activity, rather than as a splintered set of individual ones. All could be used as part of other activities and should not be isolated so that centering becomes a distinct part of the class schedule. As the teacher begins to explore the possibilities for using centering within the class, it will probably become apparent that many centering activities have long been in existence. We as teachers have often used activities for one purpose and then have been amazed to find that other benefits can be derived from these same activities. The exploration of these other possibilities plus the development of new activities will make centering an invaluable part of the daily routine. Teachers may soon learn that they will not want to teach without centering!

APPLICATION

Case Study

Audience. Students chosen for this study were fifth and sixth graders in a low ability language class taught by a regular class teacher, an aide, and a special educator, Ms. Lee Mertz. Of the twenty-one students, fourteen had been diagnosed as needing special help and were being given outside help for low achievement, speech, learning disabilities, behavioral problems, or bilingual problems. Most of the students had been diagnosed as having low self-esteem.

Purpose. Centering activities were chosen to become a part of the regular teaching and were incorporated to stimulate self-expression, build awareness and self-control, and develop a more positive self-image.

Design. During the fall, students participated in seven centering activities and were asked to evaluate each activity at the end. No names were used in this evaluation; students were simply asked to rate the activity on a scale of zero to ten with ten being the highest.

All lessons started with relaxation exercises in which students were helped to clear their minds and to relax their bodies. Students were instructed to leave their names off the activities, and words were spelled at their request. Work was neither graded nor corrected, although papers were used to identify skills that the group as a whole needed.

Sources for the activities were *The Centering Book, The Second Centering Book,* and *A Peaceable Classroom.*

Activity 1. "The Memory Trip" from *A Peaceable Classroom* (Harmin & Sax, 1977, p. 38): This activity was used as an introduction to relaxation and visual imagery. Students first discussed the hectic pace of the daily routine and how this pace interfered with good thinking. Then, using relaxation techniques, the teacher led the students to quiet their bodies and to clear their minds. Students were told to relive their day by making a movie in their heads. After a discussion about focusing on the positive happenings rather than the negative ones, students were asked to write five sentences about the good things that had happened to them that day.

Activity 2. "Dream Completion" from *The Centering Book* (Hendricks & Wills, 1975, pp. 53–93): Students started this activity by reviewing the relaxation and visual imagery used in Activity 1. Then the teacher led them verbally through climbing some stairs and called attention to all of their senses (sight, hearing, feelings, and smell). They were then asked to describe the climb up the stairs and to tell where the stairs had led them.

Activity 3. Emotional Awareness and Expression from *A Peaceable Classroom* (Harmin & Sax, 1977, p. 40): After quieting their bodies and clearing their minds, students were led in a discussion of how our bodies react to love, anger, fear, and hate. Afterwards, students were given a worksheet and asked to draw one line to show what each emotion was like. Students were then asked to write when they felt that emotion and how they feel when they have it.

Activity 4. "What's on Your Mind?" from *A Peaceable Classroom* (Harmin & Sax, 1977, pp. 37 & 62): Students were given a sheet of unruled paper and were told to doodle, draw, or write about whatever was on their minds at the time. Next they were given worksheets with a wheel divided into four parts and were asked to write a word in each section about one thought. Then, in the space at the bottom of the worksheet, students were told to write about one of the four thoughts identified.

Activity 5. "Sharing and Receiving Positive Strokes" from *The Second Centering Book* (Hendricks & Roberts, 1977, p. 125): The teacher began with a discussion of how people usually discount compliments and led toward ways we can accept them. Students then discussed how to give a compliment, especially those not dealing with physical features ("Gee you look nice today!"). The students then chose to work with two others that they felt comfortable with and took turns giving and receiving compliments. At the end, students completed a questionnaire designed by the teacher that focused on things like what the student was good at doing, ways in which the student was improving, likes of the student, or good feelings about him/herself.

Activity 6. "Storytelling" from *The Centering Book* (Hendricks & Wills, 1975, p. 160): The teacher read the story of "The Man, the Snake, and the Stone" to the class. Students were then told to write their own ending to the story, telling what the student thought the man's future would be.

Activity 7. Three Options. Students were given a choice of one of the following three activities after completing the usual relaxation exercises:

1. *The Centering Book,* (Hendricks & Wills, 1975, Chapter 5): Write about a dream you have had.
2. *The Centering Book,* (Hendricks & Wills, 1975, Chapter 5): Write about a dream you have had in which you were falling. Describe your fall and where you landed.

3. *The Second Centering Book,* (Hendricks & Roberts, 1977, Shields and Coats of Arms, p. 213 and pgs. 202–204): Using the lists from the text, the group discussed qualities they thought were important for people to have. Then the students drew symbols or wrote words on the worksheet to represent the qualities they had identified.

Evaluation. The students rated each of the activities according to their preferences. Although a wide discrepancy was shown among the activities, all but one student rated at least two of the activities as a ten (highest). One student rated all the activities above five. The average rating for each of the activities was: Activity 1—9.4; Activity 2—8.9; Activity 3—8.4; Activity 4—8.1; Activity 5—8.5; Activity 6—7.8; and Activity 7—8.3. The overall average for the activities was an 8.5.

At the end of the project, students were given an evaluation form to complete. Again, no names were used. The activities the students liked best were those dealing with dreams. All of the twenty-one children felt they had done well on the lessons and eighteen stated that they used the relaxation exercises at other times outside of class.

Comments from students included: "I liked making the movie in my head"; "I liked telling about my feelings"; "They were about me"; "I liked them because it made me think"; "We got to draw some and I like to draw"; and "We got to just write what we thought without all the rules."

An evaluation of the project by the teacher proved very positive, noting that there was a sharp decrease in the number of student comments about not knowing what to write. Students were enthusiastic about the activities and eventually reacted positively just because they were doing centering activities. The teacher felt that the students improved in self-control, and behavior management within the class became easier.

Some of the students wrote freely about themselves and revealed aggressions, fears, and anxieties about which the teacher had been unaware. There seemed a general willingness and even eagerness to write on the part of the students. They all indicated that at least some of the activities were of interest to them.

The fact that eighteen of the twenty-one students were using relaxation exercises outside of class was impressive to the teacher, because this had been done entirely on student initiative. Students volunteered discussion about the situations at home and at school in which they used the centering activities. Most importantly, all of the students reported that they felt good about their abilities during the centering activities.

REFERENCES

Cratty, B.J., *Adapted Physical Education for Handicapped Children and Youth*. (Denver: Love Publishing Company, 1980).

Harmin, M., and S. Sax, *A Peaceable Classroom*. (Minneapolis: Winston Press, Inc., 1977).

Hendricks, G., and R. Wills, *The Centering Book*. (Englewood Cliffs, New Jersey, Prentice-Hall, Inc., 1975).

Hendricks, G., and T. Roberts, *The Second Centering Book*. (Englewood Cliffs, New Jersey: Prentice-Hall, Inc., 1977).

Logsdon, B.J., and K.R. Barrett, *Ready? Set . . . Go!* (Bloomington, Indiana: National Instruction Television Center, 1969).

10

centering and reading

Margaret A. Bacon, Ed. D.

Mike brings his reader up to the circle of chairs for the daily ritual, hoping the teacher overlooks him when it comes time to read aloud. She doesn't, and he painstakingly sounds out, word by word, the symbols on the page. He shuffles his feet, sighs, stutters, repeats words, leaves out words —what he produces resembles only slightly the rhythms and meanings of the language.

The reading teacher is conducting a discussion of a story about two children lost in a blizzard with her Florida class. The children remember the characters' names and what happened to them, but they draw a blank when she asks: "How did the children feel? How would you feel if you were lost in a blizzard?"

Incidents like these occur daily in classrooms across the country in the name of reading instruction. The problems we face in reading today are certainly *not* a result of lack of attention to reading in the curriculum. Public awareness of and concern with students' reading has fostered a national preoccupation with the teaching of reading. Government-funded efforts have contributed millions of dollars toward improving literacy in the United States. Teachers spend countless hours in university courses and inservice sessions trying to improve their knowledge of reading and reading methodology.

The result of all this concern, money, and education has been a focus on only part of the problem. Most approaches to solving the reading problem fail to deal with affective variables in reading. By concentrating solely on the cognitive aspects of the reading task they leave the affective aspects untapped and undeveloped. Surely if Mike learned to relax and approach print from a centered position, his oral reading would improve. The discussion conducted by the reading teacher would be immensely more productive if, prior to reading the story, she had conducted a fantasy journey through a blizzard with the children, encouraging them to use their powers of imagination to create the feel, smell, sight, sound, and other sensations of the experience.

Centering activities are now finding a place right next to basal readers and workbooks in reading instruction. Some current theories view reading as an active process in which a reader tries to reconstruct a message from an author. The reader brings to that interaction a particular set of language skills, experiences, and concepts. The process is complicated because the author, too, has implanted in the print his own set of such variables. In order to comprehend a particular piece of print, a match between the author's and the reader's set is required. The more unfamiliar or difficult the material, and the more limited the reader's language and experience, the more removed the match becomes.

Let us simulate, for a moment, what the children in the reading group may have been experiencing as they approached the blizzard story. A slightly different piece of material will be used, of course, since some of you may already have considerable experience with blizzards. Try this:

> Previous chemical investigations have, therefore, been primarily concerned with elemental analysis and the determination of active groups which are mainly carboxyl and phenolic hydroxyls and possible smaller quantities of quinonoid and primary alcohol groupings.

How did you fare? You probably found the vocabulary terms long and unfamiliar, and the style of writing less exciting than *Jaws*. In addition, you probably lack a set of concepts and experiences in biochemistry which would enable you to connect with the material, much as our Florida students had nothing to connect them to a blizzard. And lastly, you probably were not very interested in the results of these previous investigations of humic acids, so you were not really motivated to overcome these difficulties.

When students are having difficulty with specific material, we can adjust one of the two factors involved in this process—the material or the student. We could change the material either by finding something less difficult or more interesting; or we could change the student's approach to the material by giving him or her some strategies (unlocking new words, making predictions, varying speed) or by motivating the child to read the selection.

What we have tended to do in reading instruction is

to limit our help to only one aspect of either the material or the student—the cognitive aspect. We have neglected areas within the student that might be accessible to other types of instruction. Let us look in on another classroom a mile away from Mike's to see how a shift in focus affects the situation:

> Before she begins the reading lesson, the teacher calls the group back to the reading corner, a carpeted section separated from the rest of the classroom by dividers. The students sit cross-legged on the floor in preparation for the centering activity they know is about to begin. In a calm and unhurried manner, the teacher directs the students to tune in to their centers and has them send relaxation messages to their bodies. The students then regroup around the reading table, ready to begin the day's lesson. John, who could easily be Mike's counterpart, delivers his reading in a relatively fluent manner, as do the other children in this low group.

Centering activities are particularly appropriate for assisting the student in the reading process. Relaxation and centering can help lessen the reader's tension or anxiety, particularly with oral reading tasks, so that she or he confronts the material from a more relaxed, receptive position. Guided fantasy and imagery activities can help increase students' motivation for reading a selection, as well as their involvement in their reading. Guided fantasy and dream activities provide a framework for developing language experience stories where children can see the connection between their own language and the print they read. And on a more sophisticated level, such activities with older readers develop an understanding of literary devices and literature removed from their own experience.

There are several advantages to using such awareness activities. First, they are easily integrated into a regular program of reading instruction. They require no expensive materials or aids, only a commitment from the teacher. Secondly, they allow readers to make greater use of their own attributes in the reading process. While the activities are at first introduced and organized by the teacher, they will eventually provide the student with a set of tools she or he can use in any reading situation.

A series of activities implementing these principles is described in the following section. For each area of centering activities, the purpose, the target audience, and the activities are described.

ACTIVITIES FOR CENTERING IN READING

Relaxation and Centering

Purpose. There are many situations in which anxiety and tension either create or contribute to reading difficulties for children. As reading teachers we are aware of this problem, yet we continue to focus our attention on diagnosing and remediating what we feel are the students' deficiencies, without dealing with the underlying causes. Relaxation and centering activities can contribute significantly to the release of tension and the easing of anxiety in testing situations, oral reading performance, and concentration of reading tasks. If the body is filled with tension, if it is not relaxed, the mind does not function at its highest capabilities.

Once children are mentally and physically relaxed, they are more receptive to the process of reading and the contents of the selection. If we were to sit down tonight to our newspaper, for example, we might find it difficult to concentrate on the world political situation when our bodies and our minds are still involved with the long drive home. The roads were icy, and we find ourselves gripping the newspaper in the same fashion in which we gripped the steering wheel. Our ears resound with the sound of the horn when the driver behind us became irritated by our ten-second pause as the light turned green. In short, there is a great deal of mental and physical noise interfering with our ability to focus on and understand the print.

In much the same way, students bring many negative expectations to reading tasks, such as the idea that the text is going to be difficult, or that they have not performed well on tests before because of nervousness (which causes them to become nervous and not do their best).

Because they are so vital for preparing readers for the task, centering and relaxation activies are being used as a normal part of preparation for oral reading and tests.

Target Audience. Relaxation and centering activities are useful before any reading task, but they are especially helpful for students with a long history of reading problems. Such students abound in low reading groups and populate remedial reading programs. Their oral reading is characterized by choppy, unnatural, word by word reading. Their anxiety increases with each mistake they make and is only compounded when other students correct them or supply words. Other signs of tension are evident during reading: shuffling of feet, blinking eyes rapidly, playing with book pages or pencil. Extreme frustration with the task may lead them to slam the book shut or even throw it on the floor.

The author had in a reading clinic a fourteen year old boy who displayed many of these symptoms while reading orally, although on tests of silent reading he scored at the twelfth grade level. A discussion with the boy revealed that he had been receiving help from a private clinic where his training had concentrated on eye exercises and perfect oral reading. The training, which was well-intentioned as well as expensive, had forced him to use only the source he was least secure with—print—and did not allow him to use his innate intelligence and sense of what the English language sounded like. In addition it made him increasingly anxious about an activity in which he was already conscious of doing poorly. He was a prime candidate for relaxation activities, for they allowed his mind to depend on his strengths.

Students who become nervous before or during testing situations can also benefit from relaxation and centering activities. Many of the students who come to the reading clinic at the University of Colorado express how anxious they become when they have to take tests. Their parents often feel that tests do not show their child's actual ability in the subject. An examination of standardized test scores for her or his class can also give a teacher an idea of which students could benefit from relaxation activities. Students whose scores are low for their actual reading performance level in the classroom could probably benefit from the activities.

Another group of students somewhat more difficult to identify are those who express difficulty in concentrating while reading. We have all had the experience of reading a page of print and then having absolutely no idea of what it was about. It is as if the print has gone in one eye and out the other, to rephrase the complaint of mothers regarding their children's adherence to instructions. The high school student who claims to have spent four hours reading the one chapter history assignment, the elementary student who cannot answer even basic questions on a paragraph she or he has just read, the "window gazers" during class reading time—these are all good candidates for relaxation activities. Concentration is a mental discipline that can be enhanced by an alert, uncluttered mind. Because of its connection with a student's involvement in a particular reading selection, it can also help increase comprehension.

Activities. Centering and relaxation activities should always begin with a discussion of the activity's purpose. An open and honest discussion of how tension and anxiety can interfere with our performance in reading and/or testing situations is helpful. Have students contribute instances of clammy hands and nervous stomachs before a test, or becoming tongue-tied and stuttering while reading aloud. Explain the factors that contribute to tension and anxiety, and tell them that you want to help control it. Encourage discussion after the activity as well, having students share how it helped them with the problem.

The activities themselves are very straightforward and can either be directed by the teacher as a whole class activity, used by special reading teachers in small groups, or administered individually by an aid or student teacher working with problem students.

The "Centering Body and Mind" activity in *The Second Centering Book* (Hendricks and Roberts, 1977, pp. 12–16) is useful for problem readers before oral reading activities. The activity has students concentrate on relaxing various parts of their bodies. In preparation for reading, you may want to focus especially on relaxing the tongue, mouth, and jaw as well as the eyes. As students come out of the activity, mention that they can remember that feeling of being relaxed. They can come back to it when they feel their eyes jumping over the page or their tongue tripping on the syllables.

"The Labeling Game" in *The Second Centering Book* (Hendrick and Roberts, 1977, pp. 5-7) is a useful one to help students deal with either test anxiety or concentration. In this activity, students relax and close their eyes and then try to label their thoughts as memory, fantasy, or talk as they watch them go through their minds. If the activity is used before a test it might be helpful for them to also use the words "anxious" or "nervous" whenever they find themselves feeling that way with regard to the upcoming event. The discussion after the activity should focus on the point that while we cannot actually rid ourselves of these feelings, we can recognize them for what they are and just let them float through our minds rather than control us.

"The Art of Seeing" activity in *The Centering Book* (Hendricks and Wills, 1975, pp. 35-36) is a good one to help students who have difficulty concentrating on reading tasks. In this activity students are grouped around an object and try to concentrate on just the object (a candle, for instance), then as they close their eyes, they try to watch the images inside them. In order to apply this specifically to concentrating on reading, the teacher could have students look at the page and rather than noticing the print itself, have them relax and just watch the page. Students should then close their eyes and try to watch the images or thoughts on the page in their minds. What this does, in a sense, is legitimize mind wandering before reading, helping to remove the guilt and frustration connected with it so that students are more relaxed and ready to read.

Imagery and Fantasy

Purpose. Teachers now commonly try to prepare students in some way for whatever it is they are to read. With younger children, they may introduce new concepts and vocabulary, talk about the setting of the story, or ask the children if they have ever had an experience like that in the story. With older students in a science class, they may try to demonstrate an experiment or show a model as well as introduce new terms or concepts. Good teachers on any level try to make a connection between the students' experiences and that represented in the reading selection. Since reading is an interactive experience, building that connection or bridge between the reader and an author has a great deal to do with how much students become involved with the reading, and thus how much they comprehend. The further apart the language and experience of the author are from that of the reader, the stronger the bridge that must be built.

Imagery and guided fantasy activities are ideal material for building that bridge. By involving students at all levels of their being, rather than just the cognitive, teachers are making that connection even more solid. Thus, involvement and motivation for reading will be increased.

Target Audience. For beginning readers, the activities can be used as a springboard for language experience stories in which their own language becomes the material for reading instruction. For older readers trying to grapple with literature, such activities can help them understand literary devices and be receptive to language that is different in both form and meaning from their own. Thus the student who complains, "I just can't understand this Shakespeare stuff" is a prime candidate. Of course the activities would also be applicable in any subject area where the language and concepts are difficult. Since the style of most texts is compact, with new concepts loaded in each paragraph, these activities could apply to science, math, social studies, shop—virtually any subject area in a secondary school.

Other groups of students who could benefit from these activities are the unmotivated readers who populate sec-

ondary schools in particular and remedial reading programs everywhere. These are the "can but won't" readers:
"Many of the children who learned to read in the last
decade choose not to" (Early, 1973, p.365). Most teachers
are well aware of this problem, and yet reading programs
continue to emphasize skills and ignore attitudes.

Activities. Imagery activities lend themselves very
well to the language experience approach to the teaching
of reading. The basis of this technique is that students read
more easily material that is close to their own language
and experience. Teachers usually have students talk about
a common experience (a field trip, a story she has read to
them, a class pet) and then write their words down. These
are used as reading material by the students. They practice
reading the story alone or with a teacher or buddy, illustrate them, and put known or unknown words in a "word
bank." In short, they do reading exercises with the stories.
Teachers who use the approach sometimes feel themselves
straining to provide some kind of stimulus for the stories,
or they complain of not being able to get language from
children.

Imagery activities can use the student's ability to
generate mental pictures as the stimulus for language
expression. Teachers often find it useful to begin these
exercises with a relaxation or centering activity. The activities themselves are probably best done with eyes closed
and lights off. The imagery activities in *The Centering
Book* would provide good bases for a follow-up discussion
and recording of the students' language. Since print is not
really "talk written down" (it looks different from our own
speech), it is important to discuss the students' feelings
after the experience and before it is recorded by the
teacher. The discussion could focus on the sensory images,
such as how the rose smelled or felt (the "synesthetic

imagery" activity adapts itself especially well to this kind of discussion). When all the children had expressed their images, the teacher might say, "Let's try to write down some of our images. What should we call our story?"

Once the teacher has begun to record students' language (either on the chalkboard or on chart paper), it is essential that he or she record it *exactly* as produced by the children. This means that even if the child's dialect is different from the teacher's or the expression of the images not as sharp as she would like, they are still recorded verbatim. Since the teacher is recording, he or she can provide good models for the mechanics (punctuation, sentences, spelling, and so forth.) However, there is no better way for the teacher to stifle further expression of images than to say "Why don't I say it like this? Doesn't that sound better?"

The kinds of imagery activities that a teacher can use for language experience are limitless. He or she might, for example, have students imagine their favorite food. They should turn it around several times in their head, look at it from all angles, smell it and enjoy the smell, then bite into it, savoring the taste so that they remember it. After the smells and tastes and looks are discussed, each student could draw a picture of his food and dictate his "image" to the teacher, who records it under the picture. Class or group pictures can then be combined into a book and placed in the reading center, where it will quickly become a favorite. Children begin to perceive themselves as authors. Even the nonreader has something in the center he or she can read. If stuck, he or she can always go to the author of the page for help.

Teachers have often done "imagine that you are a pencil or snowflake or cat" types of activities to encourage creative writing and been disappointed with the results. The stories seem flat and artificial or cute. Without adequate preparation, students are not clear on what is being asked of them. Imagery activities provide that preparation. But do not be disappointed if results are not immediate. The younger the child and the less his imagination has been stifled, the easier it will be for him or her to express images. With older children, you may want to have several practice imagery activities which are discussed but not written. Several books published by the Teachers and Writers Collaborative provide a wealth of ways to use imagery activities with students (see "References").

Guided fantasies are an excellent means of getting students involved with a reading selection, particularly if the language and experience of the selection is unlike their own. A sample fantasy journey to prepare students for an Edgar Allen Poe story is outlined below. Students generally like Poe once they get beyond the initial barrier of his unfamiliar vocabulary and writing style. However, while they can give plot outlines, they often have difficulty answering class or text questions on the mood or tone of the story. The Poe story chosen is one of his best, "The Fall of the House of Usher."

The tale concerns the gradual disintegration of Roderick Usher, culminating in his death after his twin sister Madeline arises from the crypt in which he has buried her. It is told through the eyes of a narrator; the reader is never quite certain whether he is a participant in the madness that pervades the tale or merely an observer of it. Themes of madness, death, and fear run throughout the story and are symbolized in the descriptions of the house of Usher itself and in the characters' actions.

The narrator, having received an urgent message from Roderick Usher, has come to visit his old friend. His first view of the house sets the tone for the remainder of the story, and it is to make students more aware and involved with that tone that this fantasy journey is aimed. Students should be relaxed and sitting with eyes closed as the teacher says:

It's a cold, dreary fall day and you are on horseback approaching the place you are going to visit. The clouds are dark and so heavy they seem to almost press you down further on your horse. Feel the cold and the damp as it chills you to the bone. You're not sure why, but you feel depressed and a bit scared. Notice those feelings inside you. Even the landscape contributes to your feeling. Many of the trees are dead and they stand stark and naked surrounded by coarse dry clumps of grass. You look down into a black pool and cannot see beyond the surface. This, too, contributes to your growing fear. In it you see the reflection of the house. It's not visibly falling apart, but seems to be decaying. Imagine what it looks like, its image distorted in the pool. Notice a growing feeling of terror inside you. What is making you so frightened? What is inside? The windows seem like eyes staring at you. The air around the house seems different—you're not sure why, but it, too, seems to be contributing to the depression and the fright. You try to shake your feeling and go inside to visit your friend.

The students can visualize through this kind of fantasy the setting of the story and be prepared for the description in the early section. Understanding that, they will be ready for the tale of increasing madness that is to follow. A discussion of their feelings, what the house looks like, and what they will encounter inside after the fantasy is over is a necessary follow-up.

The guided fantasy technique is useful in preparing students for any number of reading tasks that are difficult. Meznarich (in Hendricks and Fadiman, 1976) used a guided fantasy in an electronics class to help his students understand electromagnetic fields. They were thus prepared for the concepts and language used in the text chapter on that topic.

Teachers could tape fantasy journeys and have them available in a listening center for students encountering difficulty with the reading of a particular novel or text.

Summary

Centering activities hold a great deal of promise for helping students with difficulties in several areas of reading instruction. Relaxation activities can release students from anxiety and tension that interfere with both oral reading performance and test taking. Imagery and guided fantasy can help bridge the gap between the students' own language skills and experience and that of the author they are reading. Such strategies can easily be incorporated into daily reading and subject area activities.

REFERENCES

Early, M., "Taking Stock: Secondary School Reading in the 70's," in *Journal of Reading,* 1973, 16, 364-374.

Hendricks, G. and J. Fadiman, *Transpersonal Education: A Curriculum for Feeling and Being.* (Englewood Cliffs, New Jersey: Prentice-Hall, Inc., 1976).

Hendricks, G. and T. Roberts, *The Second Centering Book.* (Englewood Cliffs, New Jersey: Prentice-Hall, Inc., 1977).

Hendricks, G. and R. Wills, *The Centering Book.* (Englewood Cliffs, New Jersey: Prentice-Hall, Inc., 1975).

Koch, K. *Rose, Where Did You Get That Red?* (New York: Random House, 1974).

Koch, K. *Wishes, Lies, and Dreams.* (New York: Random House, 1970).

Landrum, R. *A Day Dream I Had At Night.* (New York: Teachers and Writers Collaborative, 1974.).

Murphy, R. *Imaginary Worlds.* (New York: Teachers and Writers Collaborative, 1974).

11

the centering principal

George E. Karius, Ph.D.

To be centered is to be empowered. Power is the source of self-sufficiency and self-esteem. And when touched by love, power leads to a creative interdependence with the world. Under these conditions, peak experiences come to us quite naturally and effortlessly. It is then that we see the world in new ways and discover the secrets of the universe.

Other chapters in this book focus on the contributions that a teacher using centering strategies can make in the lives of students. This chapter focuses on the contributions of a centering principal. Although schools were designed in an era when we had a limited awareness of what it meant to be human and are now, predictably, in a period of turmoil and transition, principals are still held accountable for what goes on in schools. All too often, principals are faced with uncentering forces that are impacting upon

the school environment, forces which can seriously interfere with teacher effectiveness. In many cases, these uncentering forces emanate from individuals who either do
not have a sense of their own power or have an exaggerated
need to dominate, control, and manipulate others. In both
instances, the individual involved is neither self-sufficient
or capable of creatively interacting with others. What
centering strategies might the principal use to effectively
deal with such situations?

The following broad and interrelated themes encom-
pass the strategies that are being presented:

1. Centering is as important a concept for communication,
   planning, and management as it is for focusing on the
   mental, physical, and spiritual well-being of students.
2. Classrooms, organizations, communities, and society itself
   are all expressions of our centeredness or lack of centeredness.
3. The centering principal is engaging other human beings at
   a deep level of human interaction and is contributing to the
   development of school organizations where people are functioning at higher levels of motivation and effectiveness.

To facilitate an understanding of these themes and to
highlight the strategies, case studies will be presented and
related to a basic model for understanding the perceptual,
cognitive, and behavioral processes that can be associated
with a centering principal.

Imagine a ring or circle with a visible center. Now
imagine a principal who is both the center and the ring, a
source of power and part of a network of interlocking
power. Although principals must be held accountable for
what goes on in schools, it is illusionary to assume that
the principal provides the direct link with students in the
learning process. Too much attention to the principal as

the center deprives teachers of their power. The principal must be seen as part of a network of people contributing to the growth and effectiveness of students. Yet too much attention to the ring turns the principal into a pawn. The principal must be an energized source of power who has the vision and the skills to contribute to the overall and continuing effectiveness of an organization of people. Only a centered principal knows when to be center and when to be ring, when to be a source of power for everyone, and when to be creatively interdependent with others who comprise the ring of people who make the school what it is: a stimulating and supportive learning/work environment.

ENGAGING OTHERS IN A BALANCE OF BEING AND BECOMING

Background Information
Back to basics can be a very healthy phenomenon when students perceive their learning activities as focusing on skills for the future and skills to express their thoughts and feelings in the present. The former highlights extrinsic motivation and the latter intrinsic motivation. While the two can be creatively interwoven in a school curriculum, one can also strive for a balance in terms of time spent on the task.

Case Study
Harold was having a great deal of trouble with his seventh graders. Somehow he could not interest them in the American Revolution or in the early days of colonial America. They had been told that an understanding of history was important to their future roles as taxpayers

and voters. Besides, focusing on this material was something that society expected of them.

Harold's principal helped him understand that when students could not focus on the past or future, it may well be that they have an inadequate appreciation for the significance of the present moment. She asked Harold to observe some other teachers who were having more success by using activities that had great personal meaning for students—activities which focused on helping students understand themselves as human beings. Harold observed one class that he liked very much. The teacher was engaging students in dream work. She encouraged students to recall their dreams, act them out, and discuss their meaning in terms of human creativity and wholeness. Harold became very familiar with dream work learning activities and eventually had students imagining what the dreams of the early settlers might have been like. He asked the students to wonder how those dreams might have been similar as well as different from their own. To facilitate this process, Harold had them read short biographies of early colonists and dwell on their joys, fears, hopes, and visions of the future. Eventually Harold learned that he could virtually predict the effectiveness of his teaching by noting what percentage of time went to learning activities devoted to being and becoming. By striving for a balance, and where possible a creative integration, Harold was able to be more decisive in his decision-making and more effective in terms of student learning.

Conclusion
Becoming activities compel the student to focus on future realities in which he is a member of a ring called society. While this is important, the student must also see himself as the center of his world. He must *be* a person with intuition and imagination who is capable of enjoying

life in the present. By striving for a balance, Harold was learning an important lesson about time management from his principal. Effective time management was really the effective use of energy related to issues perceived as important. There is simply more energy available to people when they are attending to their humanness as well as their membership in a particular society. What works is when you can attend to both and lead a centered existence.

CREATIVE TEACHERS;
INVOLVED STUDENTS

Background Information

It is amazing how little teachers consult their students with respect to what goes on in the classroom and how students perceive the value of the teachers' planned learning activities. While it is important to plan and to observe what a teacher does in the classroom, the most important factor is what students actually experience. The experienced curriculum may be very different from what was planned. If teachers are not to be functionaries, they must know when they are effective. There is no better source of information than the student.

Case Study

Carol was in her fifth year of teaching. Recently she had learned a great deal about the value of relaxation activities in the classroom. The principal was pleased that she considered incorporating relaxation strategies in the classroom. While encouraging Carol to try out her ideas, the principal also pointed out that some students might not like such activities just as they might not like other learning activities that Carol had incorporated into her teaching over the last five years. The principal encouraged Carol to take an experimental attitude and consider ways for obtaining student feedback on whatever she planned. Carol wanted to know more about this, so the principal helped her develop a short feedback instrument that could be used in the classroom. The principal also encouraged Carol to share the results with him. He noted that she might be surprised with some of the feedback and shared some personal experiences that helped Carol to see how all of this would be a growth experience.

When Carol indicated that she wanted to have the students tell her what they liked and did not like about the classroom, the students were somewhat surprised. They were not used to thinking this way but were pleased with the opportunity. That evening, as Carol pored over the results, she was both pleased and chagrined at some of the responses. In some cases, where she thought she was outstanding, the students had rated her relatively low. How curious, she thought, that she should be introducing relaxation activities in a classroom where many students felt under stress because they did not know the value of numerous lessons.

In a conference with the principal, Carol learned how to set goals for improvement based on student evaluations of her performance. Carol realized why she had not done this earlier—she feared the results. She heard the principal say that students would receive great satisfaction and learn a great deal by having their teacher model what it means to set personal goals for improvement. Three weeks after Carol informed the students of her planned improvements, several students came to her after class and said that it was really neat the way their teacher had made visible changes in the classroom for their benefit. Carol shared that experience with many of her colleagues. She realized that she had grown and become more professional.

Conclusion

It is important for principals to get excited about teacher ideas. It is also important for the teacher to see herself as part of a social system called the classroom. It is important for students to see the teacher as a person who cares about what they feel and think about as persons. To the extent that students can see themselves and the teacher as a cooperative network or ring, classroom climate and teacher effectiveness will improve. After some successful experiences of this kind where the students see changes in teacher behavior based upon their feedback, more open-ended questionnaires can be given to students to express what they would like to see initiated in the classroom. As these things begin to happen, students as well as teachers will see themselves as both center and ring in an enlightened play called school.

MODIFYING THE SCHOOL STRUCTURE

Background Information

Conventional wisdom prompts school principals to think instructional leadership means that they must lead the way. Well, there are many ways. As an educator one leads by drawing out people—by having them experience their ability to contribute. More and more, organizations must be focused on the strengths and interests of people. That is different from having people wonder how they can accomplish predetermined goals that may or may not be important.

Case Study

Paul was entering his twelfth year of teaching. For some years now he felt himself getting increasingly bored with the regular routine in the high school. He wanted something different but did not know what form that difference would take. He had heard about a university that conferred external doctorates to people who were self-reliant and capable of considerable independent study. In his last year of study, Paul conceived of a plan for having students focus on process skills, and live in a mini-school community where students were responsible for their actions. The teachers in this mini-school would have one day a month to reflect on what was happening and make appropriate improvements in the school program. Paul thought that this program could initially accommodate students who were having problems in school. Later, after the program had been proven successful, the mini-school could be opened to other students as well.

Paul's principal thought highly of these ideas. He encouraged Paul to make a preliminary presentation to the board of education and to seek initial funding from some outside sources. Paul did both of these things and within two years a pilot program was off and running.

Having a centering principal enabled Paul to be effective in the short *and* long run. Paul's principal anticipated potential problems with the rest of the staff. Since Paul's mini-school was different it would automatically be suspect for many staff members. For that reason, the principal made certain that the purposes of the mini-school were clearly communicated and that the benefits for students as well as staff members were understood. Visitation was encouraged. Ideas for improvement were openly solicited. Furthermore the principal emphasized how important it was for faculty members to want Paul to succeed. He highlighted the human desire to be creative and how the school system was prepared to stimulate and reward creativity. Teacher creativity not only furthered the education of students, it also contributed to teacher self-actualization. It was not long before other faculty members were submitting proposals for making the school an exciting place to learn and work.

Conclusion

As center and ring, the principal realized that for the school to work teachers also had to experience themselves as center and ring. While Paul was moving toward being the center of a new mini-school, he was also part of a ring of interdependent teachers and administrators. Those people had to see Paul as part of them just as Paul had to see them as people he cared about. By getting feedback from other teachers while still taking full responsibility for the mini-school, Paul was able to be effective. And by seeing the opportunities for themselves to do similar things, Paul's colleagues got in touch with their power to be the source and center of new and improved school environments.

REINFORCING MOTIVATION OUTSIDE THE CLASSROOM

Background Information

An increasing number of schools have children who function several grade levels below the mean in mathematics and in reading. Attempts at upgrading students' basic skills frequently fall short of the intended mark because the student does not have the intrinsic motivation to learn and overcome his handicaps. Frequently this is so because the student's homelife is either directionless or in shambles. Yet it is possible for the school to turn this situation around in a very dramatic way.

Case Study

Dick Falcon was hired to run a local high school beset with vandalism and filled with numerous students unable to do the work expected of them in various subject matter areas. These students, invariably, were educationally handicapped because they had not mastered basic skills in reading and math. The old principal had retired and fresh leadership was necessary.

Dick met with the superintendent of schools and with the school board. He stated that he would take full responsibility for improving the school's effectiveness if the board agreed to his terms. He insisted on their support for the setting up of a learning center with individual study booths and about $15,000 in individualized learning materials. He also insisted that he be freed from some administrative responsibilities so that he could go to the parents' homes and explain his program. After considerable discussion, Dick was hired and within one year had helped about fifty students raise their reading and math achievement scores by several grade levels. He had done something else, too. He had made it possible for students to take pride in their learning and in their control over the learning environment. When Dick went to the homes of his students who were not doing well in school, he insisted that the parents participate in helping their children improve. He asked them to find out what their children really wanted and then set up a system where they could earn these things. Students were to bring home a daily report card that indicated their achievements in a diagnostic, prescriptive approach to learning basic skills. They were to get daily rewards as well as a weekly reward if they performed well. Students were told that the learning center was a *work* center, and that they had options. If they learned the basic skills that had eluded them for all these years, they would receive rewards that mattered to them. Interestingly enough, one of the major reasons why the parents were so supportive of this plan was that they saw an improvement in their children not only in the school environment but also in the home. Dick had predicted that when the student was not learning in school it was probably due to the parents' unwillingness to adhere to the contracted plan for improvement. He told parents frankly that their children would have to leave the study center if they as parents were negligent in their responsibilities. The plan worked in most cases most of the time. Soon the school board was besieged with expressions of gratitude for hiring this new principal.

Conclusion
This centering principal extended the concept of center and ring to the student and the parent—students learned because they received rewards that were important to them. They were in the ring and the parent was in the center. As they excelled they realized their own power to determine whether they would get ahead in life. They saw themselves as both center and ring. And the parents? They saw themselves as part of a large cooperative ring involving the school and the home. And they saw themselves at the center of creating a home environment that would help the child succeed. And as their children became successful and talked increasingly of initiating things on their own— both at home and in the school—they realized that they had also become more effective parents.

PREVENTING VICTIM, PERSECUTOR, OR RESCUE GAMES

Background Information
School administrators frequently discover that even the best of intentions do not always yield desirable results. What counts in educational administration are attitudes expressed in skills. Just as skill divorced from genuineness is soon unmasked, genuineness without a sophisticated awareness of what can go wrong in any change effort is

bound to lead to a great deal of firefighting and negative consequences.

Case Study

John was a new principal in a large high school. It had become clear to him that the head of the counseling department was ineffective. The tasks associated with that position were not being accomplished and other members of the counseling department had expressed their repeated frustrations with the counseling head. John was determined to be helpful, but after a year of coaching and assisting, no change in the head counselor's behavior was apparent. At one meeting the counselor indicated that the position was a bit too much to handle and less responsibility would be desirable.

John sensed that the counseling head would be much more effective returning to the regular job of a counselor. He also saw some advantages in not having any counseling head and linking individual counselors more closely with the various departments of the high school. But he also knew that the implementation of a decision affecting the career of counselors at the high school would require considerable preplanning.

John informed the superintendent of his anticipated decision. The superintendent, in turn, was very supportive. Together, they made certain that John could make a presentation to the board on another matter so that the individual board members could become more familiar with the well-accepted changes that he had already introduced into the high school. Then, in executive session, the superintendent informed the board members what might be coming up with respect to the head counselor and asked if they had any specific thoughts or concerns about it. The superintendent also pointed out the probable consequences of not making a decision, including a lowered morale on the part of other members of the counseling department. The board members were informed that the principal had abundant evidence that the existing counseling head was ineffective in that role and had not demonstrated an ability to improve.

John knew that the counselor under discussion had several intimate contacts on the board of education. He also knew that several of these board members would rescue anyone whom they felt had been mistreated. Finally, John knew that one board member had taken a strong stand against many existing administrative procedures, and seemed to want to persecute the superintendent at public board meetings. For these reasons, as well as his concern for the effective operation of the school, John had anticipated what might go wrong. The fact that the head of the counseling department had blamed her present plight on the old principal and had been unable to change or unwilling to step down from the position had been an additional stimulus to action. When the decision was finally made, there was a little ripple but no big waves. It was as though the decision had been inevitable and essential.

Conclusion

While John accepted full responsibility for his decision, he also accepted full responsibility for taking all the steps to make the decision an effective one. He anticipated the possibility of having various people in prominent positions come out of their conditioned pasts and play victim, persecutor, or rescuer games. He realized that just as he was the center of responsibility in making a decision to remove the counseling head, that counselor would soon become the center of attention for many well-meaning, as well as ill-intentioned, people in positions of power. John knew that his school was in a ring of schools of which his, the high school (although highly visible), was only a part. Should the credibility of the superintehdent be reduced, John knew that his own effectiveness in dealing with new and as yet unknown problems would also be reduced. Therefore, he focused not only on making himself effective, but also having the superintendent be effective.

By making the ring effective, the center became stronger.

EXPANDING THE ROLE OF PRINCIPAL

Background Information

Leadership studies frequently ignore the constraints that a principal experiences in terms of the role of principal or the structure of the school. In many ways, the role of principal can be overwhelming in terms of the scope of responsibilities and the intensity of involvement that is frequently expected. Good principals, just like good teachers, can burn out. Yet there are options for the principal to explore, even in so-called bureaucratic organizations whose structures appear to preclude innovation.

Case Study

Julie Watson had been a principal for about ten years before she moved and became the principal of another elementary school. It was not long before the teachers realized how competent she was; nevertheless, they were really surprised during one of the faculty meetings. Julie shared with them the overwhelming number of tasks associated with her role. She also highlighted the many innovative ideas that teachers as well as students had given to her since her arrival at the school. Now she wanted to know if the faculty would be interested in exploring a revolutionary idea with her. Specifically, she wondered if there would be any perceived merit in the idea of determining how teachers and students could be intimately involved in and take responsibility for the effective functioning of the total school. She indicated that she would be willing to have teachers develop their own budgets and to run classes in ways that made sense to them, as long as they would be willing to be held accountable for all the results. The idea would require a lot of discussion and planning. She indicated that the superintendent would be supportive as long as there was no teacher opposition and parents were comfortable with whatever ideas were proposed. What happened was truly remarkable. Over a period of three years, teachers with the help of students were doing things that seemed to run counter to most people's thinking of what was possible given the complexities of managing a contemporary school system. When Julie made presentations to her professional colleagues in other school systems and conventions, considerable doubt had to be allayed. Some people even felt that Julie had abdicated many of her responsibilities, and that teachers were overworked. It was difficult for some people to understand that even though more people were assuming more responsibilities, the job of being a teacher (as well as the job of being a principal), had become more fun, required less psychic energy, and resulted in noteworthy results.

Conclusion

Nothing is impossible for centering leaders. Such individuals are very clear in terms of their purposes and powers of communication. What Julie Watson accomplished in one school system might not work in another. But then again, how is one to know? Her extensive competencies as a principal, her intuitive awareness of what was possible, and her willingness to risk and expand the context in which responsibility for a school's operation was felt, enabled Julie Watson to be effective. Hers and the teachers' effectiveness were intimately and inextricably related. A voluntary and creative interdependent system had been established by individuals who experienced their own power and ability to be the center of their world. These views are not contradictions. People who are creatively interdependent must also be self-sufficient. These views exist as simultaneous realities. Authentic communication combined with the planning of an open system had led to synergistic management. Principals can now experience themselves as center and ring. A truly creative school organization appropriate to the unending needs of people had evolved with the help of a centering leader.

SOME CONCLUDING THOUGHTS

The center/ring model that was used to analyze the centering strategies of a school principal is equally relevant for the school teacher. Teachers who are centered are empowering leaders. Given the numerous and diverse uncentering pressures in schools and society, it is crucial that students also see themselves as center and ring in this grand and mysterious universe. When schools become crucibles for leadership development, and when teachers and students as well as parents and policy makers capitalize on this awareness to be centering leaders in their respective worlds, schools and society will have made a necessary and essential evolution to a higher level of functioning.

index

Boldfaced entries indicate activity titles. Most entries in italics are games from other sources or related book titles.